T0323588

Cambridge Elements ≡

Elements in European Politics
edited by
Catherine De Vries
Bocconi University
Gary Marks
University of North Carolina at Chapel Hill and European University Institute

CLEAVAGE FORMATION IN THE TWENTY-FIRST CENTURY

How Social Identities Shape Voting Behavior in Contexts of Electoral Realignment

Simon Bornschier
University of Zurich

Lukas Haffert
University of Geneva

Silja Häusermann
University of Zurich

Marco Steenbergen
University of Zurich

Delia Zollinger
University of Zurich

CAMBRIDGE
UNIVERSITY PRESS

CAMBRIDGE
UNIVERSITY PRESS

Shaftesbury Road, Cambridge CB2 8EA, United Kingdom

One Liberty Plaza, 20th Floor, New York, NY 10006, USA

477 Williamstown Road, Port Melbourne, VIC 3207, Australia

314–321, 3rd Floor, Plot 3, Splendor Forum, Jasola District Centre, New Delhi – 110025, India

103 Penang Road, #05–06/07, Visioncrest Commercial, Singapore 238467

Cambridge University Press is part of Cambridge University Press & Assessment, a department of the University of Cambridge.

We share the University's mission to contribute to society through the pursuit of education, learning and research at the highest international levels of excellence.

www.cambridge.org
Information on this title: www.cambridge.org/9781009475921

DOI: 10.1017/9781009393508

First published 2024

A catalogue record for this publication is available from the British Library.

ISBN 978-1-009-47592-1 Hardback
ISBN 978-1-009-39351-5 Paperback
ISSN 2754-5032 (online)
ISSN 2754-5024 (print)

Additional resources for this publication at: www.cambridge.org/Bornschier

Cleavage Formation in the Twenty-First Century

How Social Identities Shape Voting Behavior in Contexts of Electoral Realignment

Elements in European Politics

DOI: 10.1017/9781009393508
First published online: December 2024

Simon Bornschier
University of Zurich

Lukas Haffert
University of Geneva

Silja Häusermann
University of Zurich

Marco Steenbergen
University of Zurich

Delia Zollinger
University of Zurich

Author for correspondence: Simon Bornschier, siborn@ipz.uzh.ch

Abstract: Western Europe is experiencing growing levels of political polarization between parties of the New Left and the Far Right. The authors argue that this antagonism reflects the emergence of a social cleavage between universalism and particularism. To understand cleavage formation in the midst of party system fragmentation and the proliferation of new competitors, they emphasize the crucial role of group identities. Anchored in social structure, group identities help us understand why specific party appeals resonate with certain groups, thereby mediating the link between socio-structural change and broader party blocks defined by their distinctive ideologies along the new cleavage. Based on original survey data from France, Germany, Switzerland, and the UK, this Element presents evidence for the formation of a universalism–particularism cleavage across European party systems that diverge strongly on institutional and political characteristics. This title is also available as Open Access on Cambridge Core.

Keywords: Electoral realignment, universalism–particularism cleavage, party competition, group identities, politics of knowledge economies

ISBNs: 9781009475921 (HB), 9781009393515 (PB), 9781009393508 (OC)
ISSNs: 2754-5032 (online), 2754-5024 (print)

Contents

An online appendix for this publication can be accessed at
www.cambridge.org/Bornschier

1 A Cleavage Perspective on Contemporary Politics

Is contemporary politics shaped by fundamental social divisions, or by the extraordinary skills of politicians such as Boris Johnson, Marine Le Pen, or Emanuel Macron, who creatively unite heterogeneous electoral coalitions based on the issues of the day, galvanized by populist or emotional appeals? Interpretations of how and why electoral landscapes in Western Europe have transformed over the past decades have come to diverge widely. Emphasizing the role of party agency and strategy, one perspective sees new parties' issue-based challenges to the dominant position of mainstream parties as evidence of dissolving links between voters and parties and of growing party system fragmentation (e.g., Franklin 1992; Green-Pedersen 2007, 2019; De Vries and Hobolt 2020). On the other hand, researchers working in the cleavage tradition and comparative political economy scholars alike highlight the role of long-term structural changes of the economy and society at large that give rise to fundamentally new conflicts across advanced democracies (e.g., Inglehart 1984; Kitschelt 1994; Kriesi et al. 2008; Bornschier 2010; Beramendi et al. 2015; Häusermann and Kriesi 2015; Hooghe and Marks 2018; Hall 2020; Gethin, Martínez-Toledano, and Piketty 2021; Kitschelt and Rehm 2023; Häusermann and Kitschelt 2024).

The former perspective paints a fluid, fragmented, more volatile picture of "dealigned" contemporary voters, to whom political actors can strategically and voluntaristically appeal by means of issues or identities (Achen and Bartels 2016; De Vries and Hobolt 2020). The latter emphasizes patterns of realignment, implying a certain inertia and predictability of twenty-first-century politics that remains socio-structurally embedded. Although concerned with the same empirical reality, these strands of literature have to some extent been talking past each other. Indeed, that politics remains anchored in social divisions does not imply that Boris Johnson, Marine Le Pen, or Emanuel Macron do not matter, but rather, that their leeway in rallying coalitions of social groups is limited by the extent to which these groups share fundamental conceptions of who they are and what they want. In this Element, we present an account that reconciles the view that the structural roots of party systems in society incite stability, and that of an ever-increasing role of political entrepreneurship, which induces change.

This section of the Element lays out our overarching argument. We follow the idea of a cleavage reflecting a durable type of conflict in which a social divide is reflected in antagonistic group identities, and finds expression in a struggle over policies.[1] We advance the idea that focusing on collective identities as mediators between social structure and political action allows us

---
[1] This definition reflects Bartolini and Mair's (1990) seminal threefold conception of a cleavage encompassing a social-structural, a collective identity, and an organizational element that we

to make sense of the apparent contradiction that party systems have become more volatile and fragmented, while at the same time remaining anchored in fundamental social divisions. A key to understanding how social structure continues to shape voter alignments and party competition is to think about party systems in terms of ideological blocks, rather than individual parties. While the fortunes of single parties depend ever more on issue emphasis, candidate image, and within-block rivalry, voters seldom switch between ideological party blocks. Focusing on alignments between social groups and ideological party blocks reveals degrees of stability and similarities across contexts that observers focused on fluidity and fragmentation fail to acknowledge.

But this view poses a challenge to established theories of partisanship: How do ideological party blocks rally specific constituencies, if they no longer encapsulate voters based in the dense partisan networks characteristic of the age of the traditional class and religious cleavages? In this Element, we focus on the crystallization of a "second dimension" of party competition that we label the universalism–particularism divide. We are interested in how durable links between social constituencies and party blocks emerge along this divide. While parties in the 1950s and 1960s routinely appealed to social groups in terms of their socio-structural ascription – think of "the working-class" or "Catholics" – contemporary categories used to accurately describe social structure in political sociology and political economy (such as "routine manual workers," "sociocultural professionals," or "non-college-educated") have become increasingly divorced from the appeals political parties use to mobilize these groups. The puzzle, then, is how class, education, or the ramifications of social status – that continue to shape party choice, as a vast literature demonstrates – translate into political alignments.

To shed light on these processes, we introduce two conceptual innovations. One is the role of group identities as the intermediate level connecting social structure and the organizational expression of cleavages. The second is to study alignments between identity-laden social groups and ideological blocks, rather than individual parties. This allows us to disentangle the increase in competition that results from the eroding grip of party organizations on voters from persistent regularities that structure voter alignments across countries and over time. Despite variation resulting from party strategy, we find that party systems are shaped by common divisions in social structure, and that similar group identities account for their translation into broader political alignments.

---

elaborate on, but links these three elements more explicitly to political conflict between parties over policies (Bornschier 2010).

1.1 Electoral Realignment or Issue Entrepreneurship?

The debate on whether we have been witnessing dealignment and the end of an era in which politics was shaped by fundamental social divisions, or whether processes of realignment between social groups and parties create new cleavages is far from new (e.g., Dalton, Flanagan, and Beck 1984; Inglehart 1984). There is abundant evidence that the traditional class and religious cleavages have weakened dramatically (e.g., Rose and McAllister 1986; Franklin et al. 1992; Kriesi et al. 2008; Dassonneville 2022). There is less of a consensus on how to characterize the post-Lipset–Rokkan age (Lipset and Rokkan 1967), especially after the rise of populism. Have the waning of classic cleavages, the weakening of the associated group identities, and increasing cross-pressures faced by voters in complex societies given way to a more individualized and volatile form of politics that places issues at the center of politics (Green-Pedersen 2007; Spoon and Klüver 2019, 2020; Dassonneville 2022), and that offers substantial leeway to populist anti-establishment messages of "issue entrepreneurs" (De Vries and Hobolt 2020)? Likewise, the literature on populism suggests that anti-establishment appeals can unite seemingly diverse coalitions of voters who have little more in common than the rejection of the political establishment (e.g., Hawkins et al. 2018; for discussions, see Kriesi 2014; Bornschier 2017). In a similar vein, influential accounts portray contemporary polarization as detached from social reality and substantive policy preferences. Instead, Achen and Bartels (2016) suggest that polarization reflects the effects of politics or partisanship itself (see also Iyengar et al. 2019; Gidron, Adams, and Horne 2020; Hobolt, Leeper, and Tilley 2021; Reiljan 2020).

The diagnosis of increasing fragmentation and instability runs counter to the realignment perspective.[2] This strand of research suggested early on that value change, educational expansion, and economic modernization are reconfiguring the links between voters and parties, rather than disrupting them (Dalton, Flanagan, and Beck 1984; Inglehart 1984; Kitschelt 1994; Kitschelt and McGann 1995; Kriesi 1998).[3] In other words, voting behavior and party preferences are still strongly and stably structured by voters' position in the social structure, but the social groups that are key to voter alignments have changed, and they relate to different parties. Although there tends to be disagreement as to the exact structural basis of the resulting antagonism (Bornschier 2018), the basic contours of the political divide that results from these social divisions are less disputed. In this Element, we adopt a broad conception of the relevant structural transformations of

---

[2] For reviews of this debate, see Kitschelt and Rehm (2014) and Evans (1999).

[3] Indeed, there is no uniform decline in the degree to which social location shapes voting behavior (e.g., Evans 1999; Knutsen 2004; Kitschelt and Rehm 2015; Marks et al. 2023).

advanced capitalist democracies, which highlights not only educational expansion and occupational change but also the feminization of labor markets, concentration of high value-added economic activity in cities, as well as the multifaceted process of globalization and supranational integration (Bartolini 2005a; Kriesi et al. 2008; Kitschelt and Rehm 2014; Dalton 2018; Hooghe and Marks 2018; Oesch and Rennwald 2018; Helbling and Jungkunz 2019; de Wilde et al. 2019; Steiner, Mader, and Schoen 2024). Our analysis will focus on Western Europe, where these transformations toward emerging knowledge economies are most advanced, and which constitutes the region most extensively studied from a cleavage perspective. Although broadly similar dimensions of conflict structure party competition in East-Central Europe, their roots in social structure are likely to be different, given differences in the underlying macro-social processes (see Section 3). Our realignment perspective in electoral sociology concurs with research in comparative political economy showing that class, educational background, and the relative position of social groups in the knowledge economy continue to shape individual preferences and policy outcomes, though in new ways (e.g., Esping-Andersen 1999; Rueda 2005; Beramendi et al. 2015; Dancygier and Walter 2015; Häusermann, Kemmerling, and Rueda 2020; Iversen and Soskice 2019). Finally, the recent literature ever more strongly suggests that subjective social status and cultural worldviews work together in shaping voting behavior (Gidron and Hall 2017; Burgoon et al. 2019; Bolet 2020; Carella and Ford 2020; Engler and Weisstanner 2021; Hall 2020; Abou-Chadi and Hix 2021; Ares and Ditmars 2023; Kurer and Staalduinen 2022). As we discuss in more detail in Section 3, these different strands of the literature concur in suggesting that, as structural developments change the composition of society, they benefit some groups more than others, providing political opportunities for party mobilization.

The literature identifies several waves through which the dimension of party competition resulting from these structural transformations gained political traction, with the New Social Movements of the 1970s and 1980s finding expression in the emergence of the New Left and Green party family (Kitschelt 1988, 1994; Kriesi 1989, 1998, 1999), followed by a countermobilization on the part of the Far Right (Ignazi 1992; Minkenberg 2000; Bornschier 2010; Häusermann and Kriesi 2015). Leaving aside more fine-grained distinctions, we use the term "Far Right" as an umbrella term to encompass parties that have been referred to as "Radical Right," "Populist Radical Right," and "Extreme Right" based on their distinctive programmatic position regarding socioculturally traditionalist, nativist, and authoritarian stances (Golder 2016, Pirro 2023). Similarly, we use the term "New Left" to denote parties that combine progressive stances on both economic-distributive and sociocultural policies. Hence, the New Left can encompass radical left, green, left-libertarian or social democratic parties (Häusermann and Kitschelt 2024).

We conceive the conflict resulting from the sequential mobilization of the New Left and the Far Right as opposing universalistic and particularistic values, as well as their corresponding conceptions of community. The adoption of these labels reflects the gradual broadening of the issues and struggles associated with the new cleavage: Originally conceived as an antagonism between materialism and post-materialism or "new" and "old" political issues and styles (Inglehart 1984), the political expression of the new cleavage has subsequently been described as opposing libertarian and authoritarian values (Kitschelt 1994), or, with an emphasis on differing conceptions of community, as libertarian-universalistic versus traditionalist-communitarian (Bornschier 2010), or cosmopolitanism-communitarianism (de Wilde et al. 2019). The integration-demarcation label, on the other hand, explicitly highlighted the transnational component of the divide, driven by the weakening of nation-states by supra-national integration (Bartolini 2005a) and the multifaceted process of global-ization (Kriesi et al. 2008), resulting in an encompassing transnational cleavage expressed in terms of GAL-TAN (Hooghe and Marks 2018). More recently, it has become evident that the "second dimension" structuring party competition in knowledge economies encompasses distributive conflicts as well (see, for example, Beramendi et al. 2015; Attewell 2021: 20; Enggist and Pinggera 2021; Häusermann et al. 2022a; Rathgeb and Busemeyer 2022; Zollinger 2022). We refer to the universalism–particularistic conflict to reflect the value-based as well as material foundations of the new cleavage.

1.2 Changes in Party Appeals and Organization

Despite providing robust evidence on persistent links between socio-structural groups and political parties, the realignment perspective leaves us with a puzzle: How are the links between social structure and political parties fostered and perpetuated in a world in which parties' ideological appeals address broad segments of the electorate, and where party organizations no longer encapsulate specific classes or groups? Indeed, those postulating the emergence of new cleavages have tended to ignore the important literature analyzing how the organization of parties has evolved, putting in evidence a dramatic erosion of parties' links to their core constituencies (Katz and Mair 1994; Poguntke 2002; Katz and Mair 2018; Ignazi 2020). This development is mirrored in a trend of declining party identification (Dalton and Wattenberg 2002). Not surprisingly, then, aggregate party system volatility has been on the rise (e.g., Dassonneville and Hooghe 2017; Dassonneville 2022), in part due to the more frequent emergence of completely new parties (Emanuele and Chiaramonte 2018).

Katz and Mair (2018: 14–15) plausibly argue that parties have evolved from being the political expression of social groups to becoming brokers that build coalitions between social groups on ideological grounds. These changes imply their declining ability to encapsulate voters in the way they did in the age of Lipset and Rokkan's (1967) classical cleavages. Historically, close ties between parties and trade unions, the church, and related social clubs had embedded voters in political networks that linked identities and organizations (Gingrich and Lynch 2019). In step with this trend, the strategic action of party leaders has gained more weight (Garzia, Ferreira da Silva, and De Angelis 2022), although the extent to which this has occurred is debated (Poguntke and Webb 2005; Kriesi et al. 2012; Marino, Martocchia Diodati, and Verzichelli 2022). Recent scholarship on issue competition and political entrepreneurs interprets the ability of new actors to enter party competition as (indirect) evidence that voters no longer base their vote choice on stable cleavage lines (e.g., Green-Pedersen 2019; Hobolt, Leeper, and Tilley 2021).

Relatedly, a dynamically expanding strand of research studying how parties use group appeals and how they combine them with policy appeals also tends to adopt a more short-term strategic perspective, focusing on individual campaigns, on appeals to voters beyond parties' core electorates, on valence politics, and typically on mentions of narrowly defined sociodemographic groups (such as "employees," "the highly educated," or "women") rather than on the emergence of long-term party–group relations or on the political construction of new forms of collective consciousness. This includes research on identity frames, which can be viewed as explicit efforts to cast grievances and issues in terms of in-groups and out-groups (an example is the discussion of populist identity frames in Bos et al. 2020). Over time, such strategies might cumulatively contribute to the formation of "groups" in the more strictly political-sociological sense encompassing collective mobilization – and this is how this work connects to our argument (see also Stuckelberger and Tresch 2022). However, this perspective is not per se at the core of the burgeoning literature on the strategic use of group appeals (e.g., Robison et al. 2021; Huber 2022).

By contrast, we suggest that a focus on the role of social identities in *connecting* social structure and partisan alignments can reconcile the seemingly contradictory findings between the long-term realigned voter–party links and an increased role of short-term party agency. To understand the success of specific group appeals used by political parties, we need to understand how voters think of themselves and of their group belongings in relation to others. We contend that appeals only resonate with individuals when they fall on "fertile soil," that is, when individuals share a collective identity, or at least frameworks of understanding and worldviews that can provide the basis for one. In that sense, studying the social structuration of collective group identities is a precondition for understanding the differential effects of politicians' use of appeals.

1.3 The Argument: The Role of Group Identities and Ideological Party Blocks

Two contributions of this Element help us make sense of the puzzling coincidence of realignment and fragmentation in contemporary party politics. First, building and expanding on classical cleavage approaches, we suggest that social identities are important to understanding how party systems are rooted in social structure. We commonly use the concept of identities to describe who we are and what is important to us. The degree to which social groups share such conceptions shapes the extent to which the framing of contemporary conflicts by political parties resonates with them. Second, the fact that allegiances to individual parties and their organizations have eroded, and the resulting increase in competition, implies that we should find more regularities across space and time if we focus on ideological blocks, rather than individual parties. In what follows, we begin by elaborating on the first contribution of our Element. Afterward, we explain the analytical leverage we gain by distinguishing between party competition within and across ideological blocks.

1.3.1 Group Identities and Cleavage Formation

The importance of social identities is implicitly acknowledged in classical cleavage accounts (Lipset and Rokkan 1967; Bartolini and Mair 1990; Weakliem 1993; Knutsen and Scarbrough 1995; Bartolini 2005b). Yet those who insist that cleavages continue to matter have not devoted much attention to answering the question of what constitutes the "glue" linking social groups and political parties. While we have learned a lot about the socio-structural groups underlying the universalism–particularism divide, as well as on the discourse of the political actors mobilizing it,[4] the link between structure and consciousness is far from evident. This is of course an idea as old as the social sciences themselves: a "class in itself" is not yet a "class for itself" (cf. Marx 1937 [1852], 192), and "categories of analysis" (e.g., based on socio-structural conditions) are potentially far from being "categories of practice" (through which people experience group belonging) (Bourdieu 1985).

---

[4] On the structural basis of the far right, see, among others, Minkenberg and Perrineau (2007), Arzheimer (2009), the contributions in Rydgren (2013), and Oesch and Rennwald (2018). On the political discourse of the Radical Populist Right, see Betz (2004), Betz and Johnson (2004), Minkenberg (2000), Mudde (2000), Rydgren (2005), Bornschier (2010), and Damhuis (2020).

There are also specific reasons for focusing on collective identities when it comes to the universalism–particularism cleavage. We argue that a focus on group identities can help us make sense of some particularities in the emergence of this cleavage. In the absence of a clear-cut link between political discourse and the markers of socio-structural position we use to describe these groups, the link between the two still represents something of a black box. This is particularly true for the (counterintuitive) working-class realignment in favor of the Far Right (see, for example, Rydgren 2007, the contributions in Rydgren 2013, and Evans and Tilley 2011), as well as with respect to recent work that relates subjective structural position, such as status anxiety (e.g., Cramer 2016; Gest 2016; Hochschild 2016; Gidron and Hall 2017; Fitzgerald 2018; Bolet 2020), relative economic deprivation (e.g., Rooduijn and Burgoon 2018; Kurer 2020; Kurer and Staalduinen 2022; Breyer, Palmtag, and Zollinger 2023), or the perception of economic and social opportunities (Häusermann, Kurer, and Zollinger 2023) to Far Right support. Why exactly do such feelings and perceptions of grievance and vulnerability translate into support for the Far Right, rather than for other parties that cater to economic vulnerability more directly? To understand why culturally connoted appeals resonate with economically defined groups, the next section draws centrally on psychological and sociological approaches that highlight the importance of *positive* group identifications for individuals (Bornschier et al. 2021; Zollinger 2022). This accounts for the propensity of the "losers" of economic and social change to seek identification based on categories that correspond only loosely to their objective social position.

The construction of a positive self-image is more self-evident for the relative "winners" of the social changes of the past decades. Indeed, in the initial mobilization of the New Social Movements of the 1970s and 1980s, personal and group identity in the quest for the recognition of difference in terms of gender, sexual orientation, as well as the free choice of lifestyles were closely linked. In a process corresponding to what Snow and McAdam (2000) have called the "general diffusion" of movement identities, solidarity with the drivers of protest then expanded within broader universalistically minded sectors of society. As movement activists flocked into the emerging Green parties, bottom-up and top-down processes of mobilization and identity construction were intimately related.[5] But explaining the inclination of parts of the middle class to vote for the New Left is by no means trivial either. While the literature has identified education and work logic as determinants of universalism (Kriesi 1998; Oesch 2006a; Kitschelt and Rehm 2014), an ethnographic approach reveals how these

---

[5] For discussions of the interaction between the New Social Movements and political parties, see Poguntke (1987), and Kriesi (1999).

groups' economic preferences are embedded in broader, culturally defined world-views of deservingness and fairness, as well (Westheuser 2021; Damhuis and Westheuser 2023).

In a nutshell, then, the key question is how the winners and losers of the social transformations of the past four to five decades see and describe themselves. We believe such a perspective can go a long way in explaining why certain party appeals resonate with specific social groups, while others fail to do so.

1.3.2 The Role of Agency

Creating and reproducing these nonevident links between social groups and parties obviously assigns a nontrivial role to political agency.[6] We believe that the level of social identities – the intermediate level in Bartolini and Mair's (1990) much-noted threefold conception of cleavages – is a good place to study agency.[7] It is here that the self-definitions of social groups intersect with the appeals by political parties to give meaning to grievances. In grasping this link, we can draw on the literature on social movements that highlights how collective action frames point to injustices and combine them with a definition of the group or social category in question (Gamson 1992; Klandermans 2001).[8] Klandermans (2001) theorizes two processes that translate the "raw material" of a cleavage into collective action. On the one hand, meaning is constructed bottom-up at the interface between networks of personal interaction and media-based public discourse. On the other hand, these interpretations are reinforced during campaigns, where social actors undertake deliberate attempts to persuade voters and where they stake out who the group's antagonists are. The latter process is crucial because the social movement literature as well as the more classical sociological literature both highlight the group-binding effects of conflict (Coser 1956; Stryker 1980; Marks 1989; Gamson 1992). Combined, these two processes result in what Snow et al. (1986) refer to as "frame alignment," meaning in our case that individuals' and parties' interpretations of grievances come to overlap. Incorporating the idea that party appeals resonate with the way groups would describe themselves also helps us understand how Far Right parties succeed in mobilizing diverse structural groups

---

[6] Research on class voting shows that agency clearly matters in that the link between social class and political behavior is stronger in contexts in which parties offer more strongly diverging economic policy appeals (Adams, de Vries, and Leiter 2011; Evans and Tilley 2011; Evans and de Graaf 2013; for an application in a two-dimensional policy space, see Rennwald and Evans 2014).

[7] See also Deegan-Krause and Enyedi (2010: 697), who highlight that political parties can make some group identities salient at the expense of others.

[8] See also Thijssen and Verheyen (2022) for a conceptualization of different ways to frame solidarity. For an adaptation to the mobilization of the far right, see Elgenius and Rydgren (2019). Our discussion is broader in that it applies to all party families.

(as emphasized in the recent literature on different logics of Far Right voting, for example, Damhuis 2020; Harteveld et al. 2022).

Both the bottom-up processes in which group identities are constructed, as well as the role of political agency in reinforcing and nourishing these identities, lead us to expect fundamental similarities between countries:

(a) *Similarities in Terms of the Raw Materials for a New Cleavage.* We start here from the insight that each individual holds multiple identities with the potential of being politically relevant. Building on Stryker (2000), as well as the classical literature on cross-cutting cleavages (e.g., Lijphart 1979; Rokkan 1999), the relative salience of these identities should determine which of them will shape political alignments. Identity salience increases, according to Stryker (1980), as individuals interact with members of the same group. Because our personal interactions are patterned by social structural position – chiefly in terms of class, education, and urban-rural residence – identity salience is not entirely voluntaristic. Instead, it is biased toward those identities that are most strongly reinforced at the workplace and in everyday life. The resulting expectation is that the grievances resulting from the transition to a knowledge economy will lead to similar identity potentials across the set of advanced democracies that we study.

(b) *Convergence of Mobilization Frames.* Framing constitutes a creative, collective effort at meaning construction. It "draw[s] on the cultural stock of images of what is an injustice, of what is a violation of what ought to be" (Zald 1996: 266). At the anti-universalistic pole of the cleavage, the Far Right has converged on a particularistic frame that emphasizes the preservation of traditional (national) communities and status hierarchies (e.g., Antonio 2000; Minkenberg 2000; Betz 2004; Bornschier 2010; Elgenius and Rydgren 2019). One of the core elements of the Far Right's ideology is indeed its nostalgic component, as several scholars have highlighted (Betz and Johnson 2004; Duyvendak 2011; Elgenius and Rydgren 2019, 2022). This discourse can be expected to resonate strongly with social groups that feel deprived relative to a supposedly better past (e.g., Elchardus and Spruyt 2012; Burgoon et al. 2019; Engler and Weisstanner 2021). Combined with the large literature that has pointed to a fundamental similarity in the competitive spaces in West European party systems (e.g., Kitschelt 1994; Marks et al. 2006; Kriesi et al. 2008; Bornschier 2010; Kriesi et al. 2012; Hutter and Kriesi 2019) this again leads us to expect a fundamental similarity in terms of the group identities underlying the universalism–particularism cleavage.

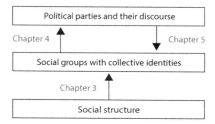

Figure 1 Processes of cleavage formation: social closure and political mobilization

Figure 1 summarizes the discussion so far (also foreshadowing the focus of subsequent sections of this Element). It illustrates how we can think of cleavages becoming consolidated. As party narratives give meaning to existing group boundaries, these politicized identities inform voters' preferences within specific ideological schemas (also see Huddy 2001; Stubager 2009). Once formed, they may also shape party politics in lasting ways as mobilization markets are "narrowed" (c.f. Mair 1997; Rokkan 1999) by salient us-versus-them distinctions into which voters are socialized. Put differently, existing interpretations of what conflict is about limit the receptiveness of voters to new political appeals. Hence, even in light of ongoing socio-structural change and party entrepreneurship, collective identity antagonisms generate a certain inertia to party system change, confining the effects of idiosyncratic shocks or individual election campaigns.

An important question concerns the proper level of abstraction to study group identities. Rather than studying broad political identities that are defined by party ideology (e.g., Sartori 1968; Bartolini and Mair 1990; Knutsen and Scarbrough 1995; Mair 1997), we suggest focusing on an intermediate level of specificity.[9] These identities – for example, feeling close to "cosmopolitans," or to "rural people" – are more specific than the broad political allegiances that cleavage theorists have traditionally focused on. At the same time, the identity categories we develop are sufficiently abstract to study the degree to which group identities antagonize New Left and Far Right voters. We elaborate on the choice of these groups in Section 2.

1.3.3 The Transformation of Party Systems and Ideological Party Blocks

Looking at the process of realignment through the lens of ideological party blocks is central to our approach. If transformations in the structure of society

---

[9] For an extended discussion of how identities can be studied at various levels of abstraction, see Westheuser and Zollinger (2021).

create social groups with a common identity, then these potentials inevitably play out quite differently depending on the specific configuration of the party system in different countries. Combined with our focus on group identities, studying party competition in terms of ideological blocks implies a higher level of abstraction that allows us to discern similar patterns underlying varying political entrepreneurship. It allows us to reconcile the structuralist core of our argument with the ever more apparent leeway that actors enjoy in tapping into and giving coherence to raw and often rather diffuse political potentials. Our contention, then, is that politicians and "issue entrepreneurs" for the most part move within the ideological space without fundamentally altering its basic contours or the group divisions underlying competitive dimensions.

This perspective is very much in line with classical cleavage theory (e.g., Rokkan 1999). It is also consistent with individual-level accounts developed by cleavage theorists, who distinguish between volatility comprised of voters crossing cleavage lines from within-block movements (Bartolini and Mair 1990). While the former indicates electoral change signaling either dealignment or realignment, the latter accounts for struggles within ideological blocks over strategies to achieve goals, the rivalries between leaders, and the disappointments that partisans may experience with respect to their government's policy record. In this way, cleavage theory has always assigned room for voters to make choices based on nuances in issue positioning and emphasis, the profiles and the charisma of specific candidates, or even economic voting.

We revive the analytical perspective of cleavage formation because it allows us to incorporate two aspects of political agency that are central for our purposes. For one thing, we seek to distinguish (a) country variation that reflects fundamental differences in the timing and the strength of the structural manifestation of the universalism–particularism cleavage from (b) more superficial and situational differences caused simply by the fact that the agents of mobilization differ by country. The prime example of the latter is that the mobilization of the universalistic pole of the new cleavage was spearheaded by Green parties in some countries and their established Social Democratic or Socialist counterparts in others (Kitschelt 1994; Häusermann and Kitschelt 2024). The impact of these differences in the division of labor on the political left on competitive policy spaces has been relatively minor compared to that variation triggered by competition between mainstream Right and Far Right parties over the particularistic potential (Kriesi et al. 2008, 2012; Bornschier 2010; Bremer and Schulte-Cloos 2019; Lorenzini and van Ditmars 2019). This is also mirrored in the far more extensive literature on strategic competition between the established Right and its Far Right challengers (the literature is too large to quote in full, but see, e.g., Ignazi 1992; Meguid 2008; Bornschier 2012; Abou-Chadi and

Krause 2018; van Spanje and de Graaf 2018; Spoon and Klüver 2020; Bale and Rovira Kaltwasser 2021; De Jonge 2021).

The higher level of abstraction in studying party competition at the level of ideological blocks also helps us to reconcile the two contrasting developments that have spurred diametrically opposing interpretations of contemporary party competition: First, the rise of instability and fragmentation due to an increasing role of agency, and second, the idea of a realignment suggesting that politics remains anchored in fundamental cleavages. While voters remain committed to broader political block ideologies, their choice set – composed of parties that differ with respect to specific issues or issue emphasis, but that align in their basic cleavage positions (Steenbergen, Hangartner, and De Vries 2015; Oskarson, Oscarsson, and Boije 2016) – expands. There is also evidence that affective polarization transcends the partisan level and divides ideological blocks, rather than just parties (Bantel 2023).

Theoretically, based on the discussion in Section 1.1, we would expect the mobilization of the New Left and the Far Right to sequentially introduce a division within the Left and the Right. Since the 1980s, Social Democratic parties have competed with the Greens (and sometimes other challengers) over the support of voters holding universalistic group identities. On the political right, as first manifested in France in the early 1980s, established conservative parties increasingly faced competition from the Far Right in rallying voters that more strongly endorse particularistic group identifications. In the meantime, as the last bastions of resistance against the Far Right challenge are falling, we see this competition throughout Western Europe. Theoretically, we would thus expect the existence of up to four blocks along the universalism–particularism cleavage: The traditional Left and the New Left on the one side of the political spectrum, and the traditional Right and the Far Right on the other.

1.4 Plan of the Element

The next section lays out how we study collective identities theoretically and empirically. It also introduces our main data source of four original online surveys fielded in France, Germany, Switzerland, and the UK. In conceptual terms, the section develops a list of seventeen social groups that we use to measure people's social identities and identifies the three ideological party blocks our analysis is based on using a Gaussian mixture model in combination with the 2019 Chapel Hill Expert Survey. Drawing on an analysis of volatility, we also substantiate the appropriateness of focusing on these ideological party blocks, rather than individual parties. While Section 2 outlines our overarching approach, subsequent sections include discussions of theory and empirics more specific to the analyses they present.

Section 3 deals with the link between social structure and collective identities. It explains why the emergence of the knowledge economy leads to education, class, and urban-rural residence constituting key socio-structural foundations of group identities. Empirically, it establishes two main insights: first, the "objective" socio-structural characteristics of voters relate consistently to their corresponding "subjective" group. Second, more culturally connoted group identities also have clearly identifiable structural roots. The section then shows how education in particular contributes to cleavage formation via culturally connoted identities.

Having demonstrated how identities consistently relate to different socio-structural groups, Section 4 focuses on how these identities are politicized, that is, which of them structure political antagonisms, especially between voters of the New Left and the Far Right. We thus switch perspective by looking at group identities through the lens of party electorates. We identify the most important in-groups and out-groups of the different electorates and show that these in-groups and out-groups are important predictors of vote choice. We also consider to which degree individual group identities coalesce into broader social divisions.

Section 5 focuses on the role of political parties in activating the identity potentials that emerge through processes of social closure and in translating them into the political realm. When a cleavage is fully mobilized, parties are perceived as representing one side of that cleavage even by voters who support other parties. We therefore study whether respondents consistently link groups to specific political parties. Moreover, in this section, we explicitly pick up the cross-country dimension. In particular, we find that voters in early realigned Switzerland have more congealed perceptions of the link between certain identities and parties than voters in Germany, where this cleavage was only politicized more recently.

Based on the findings of the three empirical sections, the final section scrutinizes the evidence for the existence of the new cleavage relative to alternative interpretations of European politics. It also discusses the implications of our findings for cleavage theory and how that theory helps us make sense of how grievances are translated into electoral politics.

2 How We Study Collective Identities

The introductory section outlined a tension between two strands of literature: One that focuses on fundamental structural transformations of society in increasingly knowledge-based economies, and another focusing on the increasing fragmentation and instability of electoral landscapes. We propose that collective identities make it possible to detect and map fundamental, systematic, and potentially durable transformations of the electoral space beneath fragmentation and seeming instability. Studying identities, we argue, is key to assessing to what extent the disruption we see in European party systems obscures and is maybe even a symptom of changing cleavage structures. Concretely, we address the question of whether a new cleavage complete with structural, political, *and* identity elements is emerging from the upheaval that European party systems have seen in the past decades. We will argue and show that a new universalism–particularism cleavage is indeed forming across various European countries.

This section lays out how we go about substantiating this claim, theoretically and empirically. We first develop our argument, highlighting why identities matter from the perspective of cleavage theory, and why a lack of attention to them represents a gap in existing work on changing electoral landscapes. We also integrate insights from sociology and social psychology that deepen our understanding of why identities help make sense of people's political preferences. Second, we describe our empirical, comparative survey-based approach for studying identities and cleavage formation.

2.1 Theoretical Argument

2.1.1 The Relevance of Cleavage Formation in the Knowledge Economy

The political landscapes of Western Europe are widely considered to have been historically shaped by a small number of key conflicts, triggered by the "critical junctures" of the national and industrial revolutions. These changed the fabric of society and became durably articulated by parties and related organizations, such as unions, churches, or associated social clubs. Building on Lipset and Rokkan's (1967) seminal work, traditional cleavage theory expanded on the role that collective identities played in this translation of structural disruption into political competition: A sense of shared identity is central to collective action, and it mediates the nonobvious step from objective group belonging to political mobilization. Strong existing identities, cemented by embeddedness in social organizations, also constrain new forms of political mobilization. They partly stabilize existing conflicts even when structural conditions change (e.g., where Catholic workers were historically unavailable for mobilization as members of the working class) (Rokkan 1999; Bartolini 2000; Bornschier 2010). For these reasons, an identity component or "normative element" became an established part of the most influential definition of a "cleavage" as comprised of structural, political, *as well as* identity divides.

Over the past decades, researchers have studied how the "old" cleavage structures have profoundly loosened, focusing on both structural and political change, but largely neglecting the question of how voters perceive their place in this transformed landscape. We place identities center stage in the study of contemporary politics. Taking traditional cleavage theory as a starting point, we conceptualize collective identities as located at an intermediary level between structure and politics (Bartolini and Mair 1990; Bartolini 2005b; Bornschier 2010; Bornschier et al. 2021; Zollinger 2024). Cleavages become consolidated at the identity level as conflict potentials arising from social structure become activated by political actors.

Much existing work points to new potentials for conflict emerging from the structural shift from an industrial to a knowledge society, which we treat as similarly disruptive as the Lipset–Rokkanian "revolutionary" junctures. While the cleavages which characterized West European party systems for decades have lost much of their structuring power, new tensions have arisen from rapid educational expansion, occupational change, feminization of labour markets, concentration of high value-added economic activity in cities, and exposure to the multifaceted process of globalization (Kitschelt 1994; Oesch 2006a; Kriesi et al. 2008; Stubager 2008; Bornschier 2018; Hooghe and Marks 2018; Iversen and Soskice 2019; Garritzmann, Häusermann, and Palier 2022a; Hall 2022). These developments change the composition of society, and they benefit some groups more than others (e.g., the higher educated compared to the lower educated; or workers in knowledge-intensive and creative jobs compared to those in routine work). They do so materially, but also more broadly in terms of status, outlook, or the rise and demise of worldviews and ways of life (Cramer 2016; Gest 2016; Hochschild 2016; Gidron and Hall 2017; Fitzgerald 2018; Kurer 2020; Bolet 2021; Kurer and Van Staalduinen 2022; Häusermann, Kurer, and Zollinger 2023).

While the timing, strength, and scope of structurally driven societal change has differed across Western Europe, these countries can today broadly be classified as postindustrial, globally integrated, knowledge-based economies. In other words, the "raw material" for a new cleavage (or cleavages) in terms of structural divides has likely emerged across these contexts. In all these countries, structural transformations of social patterns and norms have raised questions related to cultural liberalism and changing gender roles, immigration and multiculturalism, minority rights, or the boundaries of community. These topics have by now been widely taken up by socially liberal parties (especially the Greens) and nativist parties (especially Far Right, but also established conservative parties).

While some have studied the rise of the Far Right and green/left-libertarian parties from the vantage point of political entrepreneurship, the literature on electoral realignment provides a basis for thinking about them as expressions of a new cleavage. This literature links newly arising issue conflicts to the structural changes previously outlined, tracing the emergence of stable new alignments between voters and parties. By now, most observers of party system change in Western Europe will agree on the emergence of a "second dimension" of politics (clearly distinct from the traditional class cleavage), centered around predominantly sociocultural questions of individual liberties, societal organization, and community boundaries. In mobilizing this conflict, parties of the New Left and the Far Right garner disproportionate support, respectively, among a highly educated "new" middle class versus among lower-educated members of the working and "old" middle class (Kitschelt 1994; Kriesi et al. 2008; Bornschier 2010; Gingrich and Häusermann 2015; Häusermann and Kriesi 2015; Hooghe and Marks 2018; Oesch and Rennwald 2018; De Wilde et al. 2019).

There is cross-country variation regarding exactly how the structural "raw material" has been mobilized, issues bundled and politicized, and how strongly new conflicts have gained expression within party systems. The literature identifies several waves in which the "universalism–particularism" dimension gained political traction, with the New Social Movements of the 1970s and 1980s finding expression in the emergence of the New Left and Green party family, followed by countermobilization driven by the Far Right (e.g., Häusermann and Kriesi 2015). These waves of mobilization and countermobilization have played out somewhat differently across countries: especially the conditions for new party entry are well-known to differ (De Vries and Hobolt 2020); established parties on the Left did not equally adopt universalist positions early on (Kitschelt 1994; Rennwald and Evans 2014); Far Right countermobilization varied across countries in terms of strength and timing (Carter 2005; Kriesi et al. 2008;); and varying reactions from mainstream right parties to Far Right mobilization have also impacted the salience of second dimension issues (Meguid 2008; van Spanje 2010; Bornschier 2012; Abou-Chadi and Krause 2018;).

We contend that bringing in the identity element is crucial to looking past such country variation, and ultimately to assessing whether a new cleavage is emerging. An identity perspective can shed light on the "stickiness" of new group-party alignments, as well as provide important insights into what motivates voters in terms of their perceptions and worldviews.

2.1.2 Identity and Cleavage Formation in Contexts of Realignment

Conceptualizing collective identities as located on an intermediary level between structure and political agency allows us to avoid structural determinism without viewing social identities as entirely socially constructed. It is especially important to make clear that subjective notions of group belonging need not correspond to the objective (educational, class, etc.) categories with which political scientists typically operate. This point also relates directly to a long-standing debate about whether the drivers of political transformations are primarily "economic" or "cultural" (cf. Manow 2018; Norris and Inglehart 2019): identities can provide the link from conflicts between (objectively defined) "winners" and "losers" of the knowledge economy to what can (mistakenly, we believe) be taken for "mere" culture wars or identity politics conjured up by political elites. To theorize which types of identity contrasts are likely to inform voters' worldviews and preferences, complementing cleavage theory with insights from sociological and social psychological work on identities is insightful.

Sociologists in Weberian or Bourdieusian traditions have shown how groups monopolize privileges and resources by constructing "symbolic boundaries" of who belongs and who does not (Lamont 2000; Lamont and Molnar 2002; Savage et al. 2013; Ridgeway 2019; Damhuis 2020; Westheuser 2021; also see Bartolini 2005b). Material interests can motivate the drawing of (cultural, moral) in-group and out-group boundaries, but so can the quest for maintaining dignity and status. In this vein, especially ethnographic work in the past years provides key insights into the specific group understandings around which a new cleavage may well crystallize: pride in national or rural communities, identification with hard work, or adherence to traditional, conservative, more patriarchal moral standards of success provide a path to positive identity even for objective "losers" of economic and social change (the lower-educated, routine workers, etc.) (Cramer 2016; Hochschild 2016; Damhuis 2020; Westheuser 2021). By contrast, cultural capital is becoming increasingly associated with the cosmopolitan, urban, culturally diverse lifestyles and consumption patterns of the highly educated middle class (Florida 2012; Savage et al. 2013; Flemmen, Jarness, and Rosenlund 2019).

Social psychology further provides rich insights into individual-level psychological motivations of identity formation. Work building on social identity theory documents people's innate tendency to simplify the social world by categorizing and stereotyping into "us" and "them." A psychological desire to positively distinguish one's own group fosters in-group bias and the derogation of out-groups (Tajfel and Turner 1979; Tajfel 1981; Huddy 2001; Roccas and Brewer 2002; Stubager 2009; Mason 2018; Mason and Wronski 2018). This aligns, in many ways, with sociological work concerned with the status concept (Lamont 2000; Shayo 2009; Zollinger 2022). Similarly, recent social psychological work that documents identity sorting and reduced "identity complexity" chimes with a notion from cleavage theory (Roccas and Brewer 2002; Mason 2018): a lack of cross-cutting identities (e.g., today, if educational, class, and geographical divides align) intensifies identity conflict (Bornschier et al. 2021). This body of work especially highlights the affective component of identity antagonisms, which has recently entered issue-based/spatial accounts of political conflict via the concept of "affective polarization" (Iyengar, Sood, and Lelkes 2012; Gidron, Adams, and Horne 2020; Reiljan 2020; Wagner 2021; Hobolt, Leeper, and Tilley 2021; Hegewald and Schraff 2022).

Integrating these various strands of work results in a model of voting behavior in which cleavage identities mediate between individuals' socio-structural position and their political behavior. Both in-groups and out-groups are relevant here, as are cognitive and affective aspects of group identification. These subjective self-perceptions correspond imperfectly to objective group belonging, because they serve the social and psychological goals of orientation and a positive self-understanding in a changing world. Identities thus conceptualized provide an entry for studying the "glue" of cleavage formation in the twenty-first-century knowledge economy environment. Comparing against the most pillarized, encapsulated, formally organized manifestations of traditional cleavages, stable and recurring patterns of electoral realignment in today's fast-paced, individualized, politically volatile societies are somewhat puzzling at first glance. Indeed, the decline in actual *partisan* identity (not to mention party membership) is a key factor that complicates the study of contemporary cleavages. Our expectation is that studying the intermediary level of identities can reveal regularities and cross-national patterns that are hidden when looking at voting and partisanship alone. We expect voters to have a clearer understanding of the *broader* political blocks or camps where "people like them" belong (or *do not* belong) politically. Group identities that clearly link structural divides in the knowledge economy to political options that represent universalism versus particularism would be strongly indicative of a new, fully-fledged cleavage taking shape.

2.2 Empirical Strategy

2.2.1 Survey Design

To study identities associated with a universalism–particularism cleavage, we fielded a bespoke online survey in France, Germany, Switzerland, and the UK. The surveys were implemented by the survey company Bilendi between November 2020 and January 2021. We recruited 2,000 participants each in France and Germany and 3,000 participants each in Switzerland and the UK. In Switzerland, we only recruited participants from the German and French speaking parts. In the UK, we only recruited participants from England, to avoid capturing conflicts over national identity (Scottish, Welsh, etc.) more specific to the UK context. The samples are population-representative in terms of education, age, and gender.

We selected these four countries because they are part of the same historical area of political cleavage formation but are at different stages of electoral realignment. While France and Switzerland are representative of countries that experienced early and strong realignment, Germany and the UK are cases of late and less consolidated realignment (Kriesi et al. 2008; Bornschier 2012). The former two countries saw the early establishment of a strong "particularist" Far Right. Switzerland's major left parties further jointly represent a particularly extreme articulation of the "universalist" New Left side of a new divide (Rennwald and Evans 2014; Bornschier et al. 2021). Meanwhile, the Far Right in Germany made a much later breakthrough (including for institutional and historical reasons), and in the UK, the party system constrained the articulation of new divides in the political arena (although the Brexit referendum seems to have been a substitute and catalyst in this respect, cf. Hobolt, Leeper, and Tilley 2021).

Importantly, despite this variation in party system change, the structural transformations expected to generate new identity potentials have occurred in all four countries. The fact that the last bastions of resistance against the Far Right have fallen in most Western European party systems suggests that the space for political agency is limited, certainly in fully preventing the emergence of this divide. The strategic action of established political parties helps explain why Far Right parties were able to break into party systems earlier in places like France, Switzerland, Flanders, and the Netherlands, and much later in Germany, Britain, as well as a parts of Southern Europe. As a result, the electoral realignment of educational groups or classes along the second dimension, shifts of dimension salience, and the association of specific bundles of issues with New Left and Far Right parties is more entrenched in some countries than others (differences we address in Section 5). However, while their political expression may vary somewhat, we expect to see similar identity divides anchored in structural divisions across all four countries.

In the survey, we ask respondents about their sociodemographic characteristics, political attitudes, and party preferences. However, the center piece of the survey are novel questions on group identity (building on Bornschier et al. 2021). We work mainly with a series of closed-ended questions in which we ask respondents about perceived closeness to different social groups ("Of the following groups, how close do you feel towards them? By 'close' we mean people who are most like you in terms of their ideas, interests, and feelings."), on a ten-point scale ranging from "not at all close" to "very close." We consider this survey item a good starting point to extend research in cleavage theory to encompass group identities. The validation of this measure is discussed extensively in the appendix to Section 2.

2.2.2 Selection and Measurement of Identities

The survey asked about belonging to seventeen specific groups, in randomized order. Our aim was to tap into group categories that are closer to the structural foundations of a new divide according to the literature (education, class, place of residence) and others that are closer to the sociocultural distinctions through which these divides become manifest (e.g., conationals versus cosmopolitans). We also aimed to include both identities theorized to be newly emerging and others that were already associated with traditional cleavages. In selecting group categories and developing the wordings, we drew inspiration from qualitative work (e.g., Lamont 2000; Savage 2015; Cramer 2016), built on a previous Swiss study (Bornschier et al. 2021), and on results from open-ended survey questions (Zollinger 2024).

Concretely, the survey asked about the following groups (the distribution of responses is shown in appendix Figure A2.2):

- Education: We use three categories, namely, *people with a higher education degree, people with medium-level education* (*vocational training* in Germany and Switzerland), and people with *lower-level education*. Already associated with traditional class divides (Bourdieu 1984), education has become recognized as the primary structural divide underpinning a new universalism–particularism conflict, especially in knowledge-based economies (Stubager 2008; Kriesi et al. 2008; Iversen and Soskice 2019).
- Class: To tap into the traditional vertical class dimension, we asked respondents how close (or distant) they felt to *wealthy people* and *people with humble financial means*. Targeting more horizontal class divisions (Oesch 2006b; Savage et al. 2013) as well as work more versus less associated with the knowledge economy, we further asked about *people who do hard, tiring work*, *people who do creative work*, and *people who work in the social and education sector*.
- Residence: We asked about closeness to *urban* and *rural people*, given the geographical dimension of emerging divides in the knowledge society (Cramer 2016; Fitzgerald 2018; Maxwell 2019; Iversen and Soskice 2019; Patana 2022).
- National (nativist) identity: The survey asked about closeness to *German/ Swiss/French/British people* and about closeness to *people with a migration background*. Asking about people with a migration background also allows us to partly tap the ethnic and racial component of divides over diversity in a European context.

- Parochialism/communitarianism versus universalism/cosmopolitanism: Here, we asked about *cosmopolitans* and *people who are down-to-earth and rooted to home*. We further asked about self-perceived belonging to *culturally interested people*, given milieu studies that indicate "cultural capital" becoming increasingly linked to cosmopolitan (urban) lifestyles (Savage 2015; Flemmen, Jarness, and Rosenlund 2019).
- Gender/Feminism: An item about closeness to *feminists* is designed to capture the gender component of new conflicts, with especially the women's movement having contributed to the emergence of the New Left.
- Religion: Lastly, we ask about *closeness to people with Christian-Western values*. Traditionally associated with the religious cleavage and Christian Democracy, transformed aspects of this divide could also feed into a newer universalism–particularism divide.

Throughout this Element, the following groups will turn out as differentiating most effectively between the two extremes of the universalism–particularism dimension: nationals, people with a migration background, cosmopolitans, and people who are down-to-earth and rooted to home. We will therefore zoom in on these groups in many of the analyses. Further items designed around the related concepts of identity, social closure, and political mobilization inquired into respondents' networks or social interactions, perceived overlaps between different types of group boundaries, or voters' associations of groups with specific parties. The survey also included a conjoint experiment that asked respondents to choose identity profiles to which they felt closer. The exact wording and operationalization of identity-related concepts based on these items will be detailed in the subsequent sections, along with the presentation of results.

2.2.3 Identification and Operationalization of Party Blocks

As already explained, our aim in studying collective identities is partly to look beyond country specificities in party competition to common patterns of cleavage formation. We are not primarily interested, for instance, in the role that social democratic (versus Green/left-libertarian parties) play in mobilizing the universalist side of a cleavage; or in whether a *specific* mainstream conservative party dabbles in the particularist Far Right field. Our interest lies in more overarching identity divides that provide voters with the cues of where they belong in the political landscape.[10]

---

[10] This relates to recent work in the literature on affective polarization (Bantel 2023). We think of broader social (not partisan) identities as underpinning positive/negative affect toward ideological blocks.

Following this logic, we investigate the political articulation of a new cleavage from a perspective of party blocks. We derive these blocks empirically and validate them theoretically. Starting from an empirical classification makes sense here because, as mentioned, parties' ideological positions matter more than their belonging to historically grown party families. Our party classification is based on mixture models fitted to the 2019 Chapel Hill Expert Survey (CHES) data on all Western and Southern European countries, excluding Eastern Europe. The mixture model allows for a clear identification of clusters and their structures based on the Bayesian Information Criterion (BIC). Moreover, it probabilistically assigns parties to clusters, which makes it easier to handle parties with amorphous profiles.

We proceed in two steps: First, based on the economic left-right and GAL-TAN dimensions of the CHES, we start with an initial clustering of parties. As per the BIC, this results in three clusters: one that is economically and socially left-wing, one that is economically right-wing and socially progressive, and another that is economically right-wing and socially conservative (roughly conforming to a tripolar model of the political space, but with the third cluster reaching beyond what is typically discussed as the Far Right party family). In a second step, we refine each first-stage cluster based on the issues on which it is most heterogeneous (considering sixteen issues available in the CHES). Note that the BIC does not indicate sub-clustering to be necessary for all first-stage clusters, but we consider within-cluster differences to gain further insights. This second step produces six narrower clusters:

1. Green left, consisting of pro-environmental, economically left, and culturally progressive parties.
2. Traditional left, consisting of economically left and culturally progressive parties that take more moderate environmental positions.
3. Left liberals, consisting of parties that take pro-environmental stances, favor civil rights over law and order, and tend to cater more to urban interests.
4. Right liberals, who are more moderate on the environment, tend more to law and order positions, and have a more rural focus than the left-liberals.
5. Traditional right, consisting of economically right and culturally conservative parties. Those parties, however, favor open societies and are more moderate on moral issues than the radical right.
6. Far Right, who are economically conservative, favor a closed society, and traditional mores.

In subsequent analyses, we focus on three party blocks based on this differentiated perspective: one based on the Far Right cluster, one on the traditional

Table 1 Classification of parties into party blocks

Party blocks	CH	DE	FR	UK
New Left	SP, GPS, PdA, AL	SPD, die Grünen, die Linke, Piratenpartei	EELV, PS, LO, NPA, FI	Labour, Greens, LibDem
Right	FDP, CVP, BDP, CSP, EVP	CDU/CSU	LR, DLF	Conservatives
Far Right	SVP, Lega, EDU	AfD, NPD	RN	UKIP, Brexit party
Right Liberal	–	FDP	LREM, MODEM	–

right cluster, and a New Left block that combines the green left and traditional left clusters (both of which are broadly left-wing economically as well as culturally, in line with the tripolar model of political competition, Oesch and Rennwald 2018). We opt to disregard the left liberal cluster (which only concerns the Swiss Green Liberals in the countries we study), and we go on to consider the right liberal cluster specifically for France, where we would otherwise exclude Macron's La République En Marche as well as the Mouvement Démocrate (MoDem). Table 1 shows the final classifications of parties in our sample.[11]

An important question concerns electoral volatility. Here, we followed Steenbergen and Willi (2019) and derived consideration sets from our respondents' stated propensities to vote for different parties (full details are in the online appendix). For each respondent, we identified the list of parties they consider voting for. We then determined whether those parties are mostly situated within one of the blocks we identified, or whether there is a great deal of cross-block consideration. Our methodology suggests that the average consideration set size was greater than one party, suggesting a potential for volatility. However, this volatility appears to have been limited. The percentage of consideration sets that included only parties from one of the four blocks in Table 1 were 66.0 in England, 73.6 in France, 71.9 in Germany, and 65.3 in Switzerland. We conclude that there is constrained electoral volatility in the four countries. In addition to measuring propensities to vote, we also asked respondents for their party choice, that is, which party they would vote for if national elections were held next Sunday. We use the latter measure for most analyses conducted in the following sections.

Having introduced our survey design and established our definition of party blocks, we are now in a position to evaluate our theoretical claims empirically.

---

[11] In our cluster analysis, the British Liberal Democrats are classified as a Left party. In actuality, it is roughly 85 percent classified in this category and 15 percent in a liberal cluster.

In the following section, we first study the link between social structure and social identities, before we bring in party choice in Section 4.

3 How Social Structure Shapes Social Identities

In this section, we argue that newly emerging political identities and antagonisms are firmly rooted in processes of profound socio-structural transformation. To substantiate this contention, we start this section by theorizing the emergence of knowledge economies and the attributes that shape opportunities and challenges in these economies. We then also briefly discuss why economic-material life circumstances are likely to shape socioculturally connoted identities, before turning to empirics, documenting (i) the structural rootedness of identities, (ii) the importance of education in structuring antagonistic sociocultural identities, and (iii) substantiating our claim about an emerging cleavage through analyses of social networks and the antagonistic nature of identity formation at the poles of the new cleavage.

3.1 Knowledge-Based Economies: Structuration and Identities

All existing accounts of the formation of a new party-political cleavage between universalism and particularism in Europe link this development to important societal transformations as key drivers of cleavage formation. A key distinction can be drawn between approaches that emphasize the role of *economic and social structural change* – linked to tertiarization, globalization or new inequalities (e.g., Kitschelt 1994 as an earlier example and Iversen and Soskice 2019 as a more recent one), and approaches that see *political and institutional developments* of international integration and the weakening of the nation-state as crucial in this process (e.g., Bartolini 2005a or Hooghe and Marks 2018). As we explain in this section, our perspective is closer to the former approach. We insist on the emergence of the knowledge economy as the main structural driver of political realignment. While the politicization of borders and immigration is clearly a very important dimension of current cleavage formation, the focus on international integration and the nation-state alone cannot account for the fact that universalistic and particularistic voters and parties diverge on many additional issues that are not related to international integration, such as gender or cultural liberalism.

Our focus on economic and social structural change in driving the antagonism between universalistic and particularistic political positions does not imply, however, that we conceive of the drivers of cleavage formation in purely materialistic terms. Rather, we re-connect with the understanding of structural change as an encompassing transformation of people's economic, social, and cultural life circumstances and perspectives – as introduced, for example, by Betz's emphasis on "modernization" (1994). Given the encompassing nature of this change, it affects both material preferences and cultural values that people hold. Related and later contributions have also adopted such an encompassing perspective on the implications of economic and social change (e.g., Kitschelt 1994, Kriesi et al. 2008, Bornschier 2010).

Indeed, socio-structural change over the past decades has been transformative on several fronts: globalization, the transition from an industry-based to a service-economy, educational expansion and occupational upgrading, as well as technological change are among the most prominent economic processes that affect all Western European democracies (e.g., Oesch 2013, Wren 2013; Beramendi et al. 2015,). They have come with deep social changes in terms of family organization, gender roles, and multiculturalism. In this Element, we refer to the *transformation of society toward increasingly knowledge-based advanced economies* as a process that encompasses these interconnected dimensions of change. Knowledge economies refer to production systems in which productivity and growth are increasingly driven by cognitive skills and tasks (Powell and Snellman 2004), usually concentrated in urban hubs. This process of upgrading and concentration – driven and accelerated by globalization, social and technological change – has deeply affected all economies in Western Europe. Correlates are a massive expansion of skilled occupations with cognitive, creative and/or interpersonal task profiles, and a progressive feminization of the workforce, but also an extensively documented decline of routine-task jobs, especially in predominantly male manufacturing employment (Oesch 2013, Autor and Dorn 2013).

We emphasize the emergence of the knowledge economy as the key underlying socio-structural change driving sociopolitical realignments, precisely because of its multidimensionality. In this sense, we are less interested in isolating the (causal) effect of a specific driver of social identities, but in characterizing the encompassing transformation of society that occurs in what Peter Hall (2021) aptly calls "the era of knowledge-based growth." From a political perspective, we are particularly interested in the *differential effects* knowledge economy development has on citizens, that is, the winners and losers of structural change.

The knowledge economy affects citizens' life circumstances not only materially but also in terms of social status and opportunities, because prospects differ for the young and the old, the high- and low-educated, men and women, native and migrant workers among other categories. Hence, across Western Europe, new inequalities have contributed to raising the saliency of questions related to cultural liberalism and changing gender roles, immigration and multiculturalism, or the boundaries of communities. In that sense, the emergence of the knowledge economy is as much a process of socioeconomic as of sociocultural transformation. It is precisely the profound reallocation of not only economic but also cultural and social capital in knowledge economies that is relevant for our study of party-political cleavage formation. The dynamics we focus on entail *equally strong economic and cultural dynamics* that are politicized.

3.1.1 Social Structure in Knowledge-Based Economies: Education, Class, Residence

We focus our analyses of the sociocultural rootedness of collective identities in education, occupational class, and urban-rural residence. These characteristics have been shown to deeply structure both the distribution of material and cultural opportunities in today's societies, as well as political attitudes and voting behavior. At the same time, their link to universalistic-particularistic collective identities is far from trivial, as these sociological categories do not directly materialize in the political organizations and mobilization strategies we observe in Western Europe.

Education is the posterchild of social stratification in the knowledge economy. To quote Hooghe, Marks, and Kamphorst (2022): "The university is to the information revolution what the factory is to the industrial revolution." Not only have we witnessed a tremendous expansion of higher education across Western Europe over the past decades – with today on average 60–70 percent of young people enrolled in some form of tertiary education in Western economies compared to ca. 30 percent in the 1970s (Garritzmann et al. 2022b) – but we also see education premiums rise across all developed economies (Weisstanner and Armingeon 2020).

In line with the literature, we distinguish lower (primary and lower secondary education), middle (upper- and post-secondary education and professional training), and higher *levels of education degrees* (tertiary education). Its close link to the knowledge economy brings us to prioritize education over narrower aspects of social stratification such as income or wealth.

Beyond socioeconomic status, the unequal occupational dynamic as a consequence of deindustrialisation and service sector growth (Oesch 2013), as well as task-biased technological change (Kurer and Palier 2019) have brought to the forefront conceptualizations of "types" of tasks and education – that is, how the everyday experience of different work logic shapes how people evaluate opportunities, and how they think about universalism and particularism.

We conceptualize this idea of milieu, work logic, or educational socialization by means of two indicators, *educational field* on the one hand and *occupational class* on the other hand. In terms of education field, we follow Hooghe, Marks, and Kamphorst (2022) and focus on an indicator of the ratio of communicative and cultural skills in relation to all types of skills in a particular education field (cultural, economic, communicative, and technical skills, CECT). This measure is based on four types of resources characterizing different fields of education (van de Werfhorst and Kraaykamp 2001): cultural, communicative, economic, and technical. In line with Hooghe, Marks, and Kamphorst (2022) we allocate the CECT value (between 0 and 1) to fourteen education fields.[12]

The distinction between occupational classes along vertical and horizontal lines (Oesch 2006b) taps into a very similar idea, that is, the everyday socialization of people through experiences and tasks. Building on extensive research highlighting the relevance of occupational classes for economic resources and risks (Oesch 2006b, Häusermann, Kurer, and Schwander 2014), as well as for preferences and electoral behavior (e.g., Kitschelt and Rehm 2014), we distinguish business owners, technicians, production workers, managers, clerks, sociocultural professionals, and service workers.

Finally, we study where people live as a key dimension of social structuration in the knowledge economy. Given the creative, interpersonal, and communicative aspect of knowledge economy jobs, it is argued that the structuring impact of urban-rural – or centrist-remote – residence is particularly strong in the era of knowledge-based growth. Indeed, opportunities in terms of employment, access to education and jobs, as well as socially and culturally diverse activities tend to concentrate in urban centers (Iversen and Soskice 2019). Hence, we also explore how urban-rural residence relates to group identities. We measure objective residence in terms of population size of respondents' place of residence, calibrated to the national context. We distinguish bigger cities (more than 100,000 inhabitants; in Switzerland more than 50,000 inhabitants), (sub)urban areas, and small towns and rural areas (less than 5,000 inhabitants; in Switzerland, less than 2,000).

3.1.2 How Socio-structural Categories Translate into Sociocultural Group Identities

In this section, we show how group identities – and in particular culturally connoted group identities – relate to socioeconomic categories of social

---

[12] The CECT values of the fourteen education fields are the following: Agriculture: 0.0000; Transport/telecommunications: 0.036; Technical: 0.036; Economics/business: 0.188; Law: 0.312; Public order: 0.494; General: 0.531; Medical: 0.554; Science: 0.614; Personal care: 0.680; Social studies: 0.861; Arts: 0.952; Humanities: 0.952; education: 1.000.

structuration. A different question, of course, is *why* ascriptive social categories relate to subjective group perceptions that do not correspond straightforwardly to the related socioeconomic categories. The step from objective group belonging to subjective identity (and eventually political mobilization) goes to the heart of political sociology and is nontrivial in any case. The link between education, class, and residence to cosmopolitanism, feminism, national identity, feeling down-to-earth and rooted to home, feeling close to people with migration background, and so on seems even more complex to theorize. However, as developed in this section, the rise of the knowledge economy has transformed life conditions, prospects, and risks of individuals not only in material-economic terms but also in broader sociocultural terms.

As the previous section argued, both cultural sociology and social psychology provide us with tools to understand why people identify with social groups that provide them with self-value, status, and a sense of recognition. Because of such motivational drivers, a new cleavage may crystallize around pride in national or rural communities, identification with hard work, or adherence to traditional, conservative, more patriarchal moral principles – in demarcation from the increasingly cosmopolitan, urban, "alternative" habitus of the educated middle class. Translating this idea to our study of changing group identities, it explains why "losers of the knowledge economy" may rather draw group boundaries in terms of cultural identities based on notions of "hard work," being "down-to-earth," or nationality. Similarly, the "winners of the knowledge economy" may tend to draw recognition and identity from values and habits linked to universalistic orientations – for example, cosmopolitanism, openness, and support for social and political minorities – rather than from their education or occupational class.

Research on the material determinants of behavior has started to integrate some of the insights on the need for status recognition and self-worth through group boundaries. One key aspect is the increasingly strong focus on *relative* measures of grievances, acknowledging that people evaluate their social situation in comparison to reference groups (Kurer and van Staalduinen 2022; Breyer, Palmtag, and Zollinger 2023; Häusermann, Kurer, and Zollinger 2023). Experiencing *relative* economic decline – or the threat of it – is indeed positively correlated with support for radical right and radical left parties (Burgoon et al. 2019; Kurer 2020; Engler and Weisstanner 2021; Kurer and van Staalduinen 2022).

It is important to highlight the implication of taking these mechanisms seriously. The long-standing debate about whether the drivers of political-electoral behavior are primarily "economic" or "cultural" (cf. Manow 2018; Norris and Inglehart 2019) has been misleading. The question is not whether people radicalize politically because they are either "poor" or "racist."

Rather, people experience material transformations of their life circumstances in a broad array of forms: in terms of opportunities for mobility, whether they are part of an upward social–economic–cultural dynamic or a precarious one, whether the world looks increasingly similar to what they are familiar with or the opposite, and so on. These very real transformations lead individuals to (re-)imagine themselves as members of social groups that provide order, reassurance, and status. Collective identities provide the link from conflicts between (objectively defined) "winners" and "losers" of the knowledge economy to what can mistakenly be taken for "mere" culture wars or identity politics. Conflict over group identities and perceptions of deservingness, fairness, or "common-sensical" evaluations entail economic as well as cultural evaluations (Damhuis and Westheuser 2023). This is likely why material compensation seems to have very limited effect on preventing radicalization among declining groups (Gingrich 2019). Identity divides develop a powerful ideological–political map through with individuals interpret the world, a map that solidifies through mobilization and representation – in short, processes of cleavage formation.

3.2 Empirical Analyses: Structuration of Identities and Cleavage Formation

In this section, we present evidence on the structural foundations of cleavage formation via group identities in three steps: First, we analyze the links between key socio-structural categories and closeness to different identity groups. Our aim is to show that voters' group identities are rooted socio-structurally. Second, we provide evidence that education is at the heart of cleavage formation. In a third step, we empirically substantiate our contention of emerging cleavage formation by looking at social network formation along identity lines and by pointing to the symmetry in the identity hierarchies of people at the extremes of the universalism–particularism divide.

3.2.1 Validating the Structural Rootedness of Identities

We start with Figures 2–4, which provide the findings of linear regression models, pooled across countries (with data weighted by education, gender, and age), predicting closeness to key identity groups by education level, education field, occupational class, residence, age, and gender. Since the "objective" sociodemographic attributes of respondents relate in a plausible and straightforward manner to the corresponding "subjective" group identities (Figure 2), we validate our measure of group identity (closeness) and substantiate that identity conflicts are tightly linked to people's material life conditions.

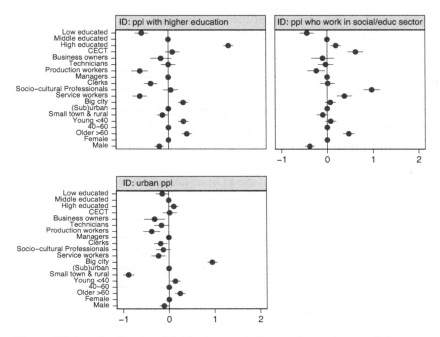

Figure 2 Education level and field, class, and place as determinants of closeness
toward groups defined by education, work logic and residence

Figure 2 shows this validation link between objective and subjective groups for three exemplary identities.[13] The level of education clearly and significantly predicts closeness to people with high education. Education also has some explanatory leverage for class identities (work in the social/education sector) and urban identities, but decidedly less so than for education itself. Rather, closeness to class identities is better explained via both field of education (CECT) and occupational class. People with a high share of communication and cultural skills in their education profile, as well as sociocultural professionals, identify particularly strongly with people working in the social and education sector. Conversely, production workers, who epitomize traditional, routine manual labor, feel most distant to people working in the education and social sectors. Finally, objective residency predicts closeness or distance toward urban identity most strongly.

Figures 3 and 4 go beyond the validation of subjective group identities. Rather, they show that *even* key sociocultural group identities are firmly

---

[13] For reasons of space, we do not show the findings for the corresponding "opposite" groups (low education, hard/tiring work, and rural people). However, the findings are consistent, with objective attributes predicting closeness to the corresponding subjective group.

rooted in education, educational field, occupational class, and/or residency. The pervasive and consistent predictive power of education level is particularly striking: People with high education feel close to cosmopolitans, to people with migration background, to feminists, culturally interested people, and to people with Christian-Western values. At the same time, they feel relatively distant from people who describe themselves as down-to-earth and rooted to home, and from people who identify via their nationality. These patterns are important because of their consistency, and because they contradict objective patterns to some extent. For instance, people with migration background "objectively" tend to have rather below-average education levels, yet patterns of identification are reversed.

The fact that CECT and occupational class show strong links to some of the culturally connoted group identities despite controlling for education level in the models shows that the immediate "task experience" (in training or work) matters beyond the mere level of human capital. CECT shows strong negative links with national identity and positive ones when it comes to closeness to people with migration background, feminists, and culturally interested people. Occupational class as a determinant of closeness shows more variation. On

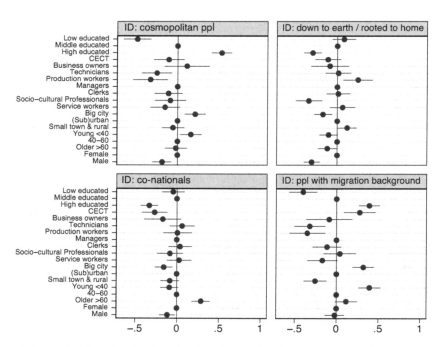

Figure 3 Education level and field, class and residence as determinants of closeness toward culturally connoted identity groups (part I).

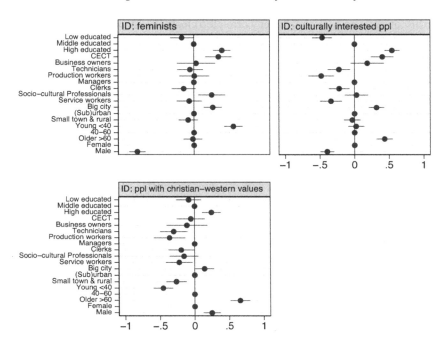

Figure 4 Education level and field, class and residence as determinants of closeness toward culturally connoted identity groups (part II).

average, production workers and sociocultural professionals appear as the most antagonistic classes, especially with regard to closeness to people who are down-to-earth and rooted to home, as well as people with migration background, feminists and culturally interested people, from whom production workers demarcate themselves. Finally, people living in big cities feel relatively closer to all the universalistic identities and more distant to all the particularistic ones. On the other hand, people living in small towns and rural areas are not clearly distinct from people in small cities or agglomerations. It seems that the identity-dividing line in terms of residency is clearly between urban residents in big cities and everyone else.

A final word on the category of people with Christian-Western values. This group identity is less clearly attributable to the universalistic or particularistic pole. Closeness to these people relates more clearly to elderly male, highly educated managers. As we will see in later analyses, this identity is indeed not part of the straightforward universalism–particularism divide but relates more closely to a traditional right-wing conservative identity.

Through the analysis of predicted values of closeness (see appendix Figure A3.1) we see that education levels predict about the same substantive effect in terms of closeness to the direct correlate (closeness to people with a high education), as to key culturally connoted groups – cosmopolitans and people with migration background.

Finally, we repeated all regressions for each of the four countries, to analyze cross-sectional consistency. Table 2 summarizes – for the culturally connoted group identities – the links between education levels, CECT, occupational class and residency, and closeness to group identities. The main finding is that we find strikingly consistent patterns across countries. In particular for the "cosmopolitan-rooted to home" pair of group identities, we find identical structural foundations of closeness in most countries. The same goes for closeness to people with migration background, feminists, and culturally interested people. For the other groups, the socio-structural foundations are less consistent. For national identities, in particular, the baseline level of identification is high, and the clearest patterns are a relatively strong demar-cation by sociocultural professionals and people with communicative-cultural education.

In light of the analyses of this section, we are now able to distinguish a set of identity groups that stand out by their socio-structural foundation and consist-ency, and which epitomize the universalistic–particularistic identity divide: cosmopolitans and people with migration background as groups to whom individuals at the universalistic pole feel distinctively closer; people who are down-to-earth and rooted to home as groups to whom individuals at the particularistic pole feel distinctively closer. In the further analyses, we will focus on these groups to exemplify our analyses.

3.2.2 The Fundamental Role of Education

So far, we have shown that group identities are clearly and substantively rooted in socio-structural categories, and that these links are consistent across a range of identities and across countries. In this section, we further substantiate the claim that education is one of, if not the key, structural basis of the new cleavage. To do so, we leverage two original elements of our survey: the extent to which individuals perceive education groups to differ along other dimensions than human capital, and a conjoint survey allowing us to show which attributes of a hypothetical person drive a feeling of closeness to this person.

First, the perception of overlaps between different divides. We asked respondents the following question: "Please imagine people with different levels of education (for instance, people with and without a university degree). Do you think these educational groups also differ with regard to the following

Table 2 The main socio-structural correlates of feeling close toward different culturally connoted identity groups

	Cultural Group Identities						
	"Cosmopolitans"	"People who are down-to-earth and rooted to home"	"People with a migration background"	"Swiss/ German/ French/ British people"	"Feminists"	"Culturally interested people"	"People with Christian-Western values"
Education group closest	High	Low/ medium	High		High	High	High
CECT correlation	Negative	Negative	Positive	Negative	Positive	Positive	Negative
Class closest	MNG & SCP	PW	SCP		SCP	SCP, MNG	MNG
Class most distant	PW	SCP	PW	SCP	Clerks	PW	
Territorial group closest	Big city	Small town/ rural	Big city		Big city	Big city	

Note: Dark grey cells indicate that the socio-structural groups predict closeness to identity groups significantly in all four countries; light grey cells indicate the same for two or three countries; abbreviations of the class coding: MNG = Managers, SCP = Sociocultural professionals, PW = Production Workers. Tables by country can be found in the appendix.

characteristics?" The response items concerned social class, place of residence, hobbies, and values. If education is a key structural element of cleavage formation, then respondents should perceive education as having a structuring effect on these different dimensions. Moreover, this perception should be particularly strong among individuals at the extremes of the universalism–particularism divide. Figures 5 and 6 confirm these expectations. In Figure 5, we see that across all countries, large majorities of respondents think that people with different levels of human capital also differ in terms of class, residency, hobbies, and values. Hence, education emerges as a heuristic associated with both clear structural and sociocultural correlates for most people.

If this association of education with other aspects of social distinction is indeed the foundation of the new cleavage studied in this Element, then it should be particularly strong among respondents with clear identities relative to this cleavage. To test this, Figure 6 regresses responses to the aforementioned question on the intensity of identifying with cosmopolitans. We measure intensity as the absolute deviation from the respective country mean. As we would expect, we see that respondents with more intense identities (both positive and negative toward cosmopolitan people) perceive the structuring effect of education more strongly.

The conjoint analysis we conducted adds further evidence to the claim that education is the key structural basis of the new cleavage. In the pairwise conjoint comparisons, we asked respondents to indicate which person they feel closer to. The hypothetical individuals were characterized by randomized values on four

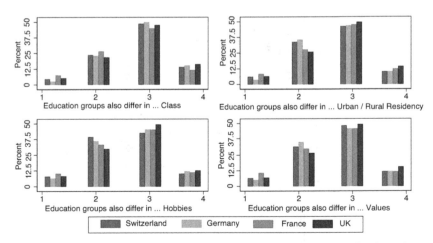

Figure 5 The perceived structuring effect of education: distribution of evaluations whether people who differ in education also differ in other structural and cultural characteristics

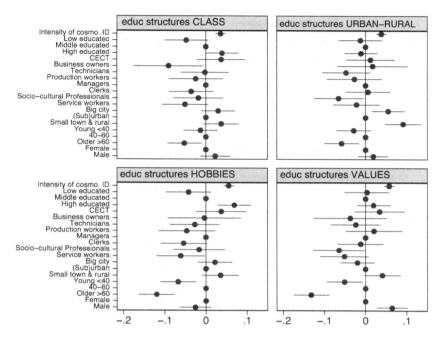

Figure 6 The intensity of cosmopolitan identity as a determinant of the perceived structuring effect of education

attributes: cosmopolitanism/openness versus national/parochial orientations; work and work ethic, reflecting different work logics; residence (city versus countryside); and the person's affinity to and perspectives on education.

Contrary to the linear regressions whose findings we show in Figures 2–4 and in Table 1, the conjoints allow us to observe the relative importance respondents attribute to different aspects of identity. In Figure 7, we show the marginal means for respondents with high and low education level. Findings are largely consistent across countries. Three findings are particularly relevant: first, high- and low-educated respondents differ clearly and significantly regarding the extent to which specific value orientations, work logics and residence yield closeness to a hypothetical person; second, despite defining the subgroups by education, values, work logic and residency yield stronger effects than characteristics more closely linked to the attribute of education itself. Hence, education is the structural basis, but it translates into different group identities. Third, when it comes to value orientations (cosmopolitanism, values, culture), the effects are not just different in strength, but even diametrically opposed. These effects highlight the strongly divisive potential of these values.

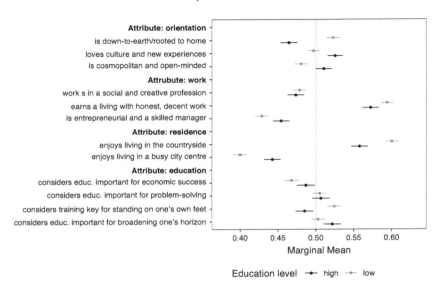

Figure 7 Choice (closeness) conditional on education: marginal means

Importantly, when replicating Figure 7 for sociocultural professionals and production workers, the findings look somewhat weaker but very similar, including the diametrically opposed effects when it comes to value orientations. Hence, we are not arguing that education level is the only relevant basis for cleavage formation. Rather, task/field socialization clearly adds to the formation of relevant cleavage foundations.

3.2.3 Evidence for Cleavage Formation

In a last step of this analysis of the structural foundation of the new cleavage, we report findings on social network formation and symmetry in the identity hierarchies of people at the extremes of the universalism–particularism divide.

A first piece of evidence for actual cleavage formation results from our analysis of social networks. Given the socio-structural underpinnings of the universalism–particularism divide in terms of overlapping and concentrating educational experiences, workplace, or geographical contexts, we expect the formation of social "milieux." Voters are socialized into social networks, develop notions of "people (un)like them," and these notions themselves may further limit social interactions across group boundaries. Figure 8 provides evidence for the formation of social milieux along similar identities. It is based on survey questions asking all respondents about personal interactions with members of the different groups we focus on. More specifically, we asked how often "they have personal

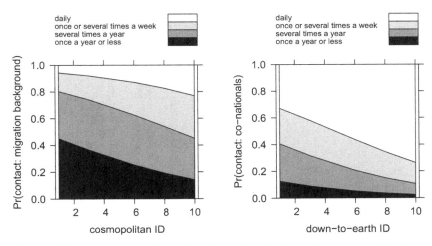

Figure 8 Social network formation along identity lines: frequency of having personal conversations and spending free time together

conversations or spend their time" with people who belong to these groups. We see that closeness to typical universalistic and particularistic identities predicts contact with people from the same category of identities. The closer respondents feel to cosmopolitans, the more they report direct interaction and time spent with people with migration background. The more people identify as down-to-earth and rooted to home, the more frequent they describe their interactions with "conationals." We chose conationals and people with migration background as network groups, as they are objectively extremely prevalent in society. It is highly unlikely that people only interact several times a year or less with conationals, or that they hardly ever have a conversation with someone with a migration background. Yet, the *subjective closeness* to these ideal-typical universalistic and particularistic identities predicts respondents' reporting and perception of their social network quite strongly.

Another indication of such milieu and cleavage formation is that individuals at the extremes of the cleavage *recognize* the other side as antagonist. This idea implies a mutual awareness and recognition of divisive values and attributes. Figure 9 presents the same conjoint findings as shown in Figure 7 for individuals with strong universalist–particularist identities. We see that the same attributes tend to elicit *opposite reactions* from respondents with strong cosmopolitan identity as opposed to respondents who identify strongly with people who are down-to-earth and rooted to home. Hence, the two sides of the cleavage indeed seem to read and interpret the attributes through similar – yet opposite – lenses.

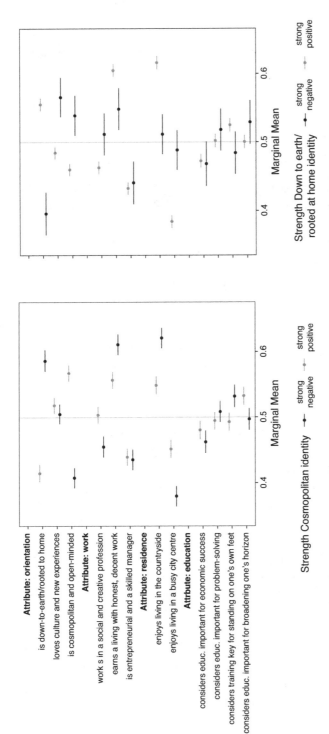

Figure 9 Choice (closeness) conditional on "cosmopolitan" and "down-to-earth and rooted to home" identities: marginal means

3.3 Discussion

Collective identities that reflect the universalism–particularism divide are by no means detached from social structure. Rather, the identities that citizens relate to consistently reflect the structural fault lines of the knowledge economy in terms of education, class, and place. Citizens' identities align with their socio-structural categories, but they transcend these immediate categories, fostering structurally rooted but culturally connoted identity potentials. The fact that we find highly consistent links between structure and collective identities even across countries with very distinct party systems and trajectories of electoral (re-)alignment provides further evidence against a purely constructivist, agency- and supply-side-driven understanding of identity politics (as, for example, in Achen and Bartels 2016). In short, identity politics is in no way the opposite of materially and structurally rooted political conflict. Rather, collective identities are rooted in, emerge from, and reinforce structural divides that characterize structural change from industrial to knowledge societies. Based on the analyses in this section, we read these collective identities as essential parts of ongoing cleavage formation, because they are so tightly linked to socio-structural potentials, relate to each other in consistent ways, and entail closure along social networks. Structural divides and the collective identities they relate to provide potentials for politicization and cleavage formation. For such politicization to materialize, however, potentials need to be linked to political behavior and organization. This is what we focus on in the next sections.

4 How Social Identities Shape Political Behavior

The preceding section demonstrated that group identities – even those that are relatively remote from objective social-structural categories such as cosmopolitans or those feeling close to their nationality – consistently relate to different socio-structural groups. In this section, we now switch perspectives by looking at group identities through the lens of party electorates. The current section thus focuses on how identities emerging from the social fabric of society are politicized, and how they structure political antagonisms between voters of the New Left, the mainstream Right, and the Far Right.

Specifically, we study how close voters of parties belonging to the blocks we devised in Section 2 feel to each of the seventeen groups introduced in that section. To bring to the fore the underlying similarity in the mobilization of the universalism–particularism cleavage across contexts, we need to approach the basic antagonisms in party systems in terms of party blocks, rather than individual parties. While our analysis mainly focuses on the cleavage between the New Left and the Far Right, we find that voters of the mainstream Right also have distinctive affinities. Moreover, due to the strength of Emmanuel Macron's movement and the disruptions it has fostered within the mainstream Left and Right in France, we also consider the Right-Liberal party family in that country.

We proceed as follows. After briefly stating our theoretical premises, we assess how distinctive the voters of the three political blocks are in terms of their core group identities, highlighting the similarities and differences across countries. We then rely on discriminant analysis to study how group identities cluster, that is, whether some of them have congealed into an overarching, Manichean antagonism linked to specific blocks of parties in people's perceptions. In the online appendix accompanying this section, we present further evidence for the relevance of identities for vote choice, demonstrating that in a multivariate setting, the most important in-groups and out-groups of each electorate constitute massively important predictors.

4.1 Group Identities Between Structure and Agency

We suggested in earlier sections that group identities mediate the link between structural change and its political manifestation, thereby bridging the view that contemporary party politics is characterized above all by fragmentation and instability, and the perspective of scholars pointing to new bases of cleavage. Building on the increasing consensus in cleavage theory that structural conflict does not translate into political conflict as a matter of course (e.g., Sartori 1968; Mair 1997; Chhibber and Torcal 1997; Enyedi 2005; Bornschier 2009; Deegan-Krause and Enyedi 2010), we suggested that the same is true for the grievances and political potentials resulting from the transition to a knowledge economy. To become available for political mobilization, social groups (or coalitions thereof) to some extent need to have a common understanding of "who they are" and, following from this, what they want. The very rootedness of group identities in social structural categories that we found in Section 3 suggests that political entrepreneurs are relatively constrained in their efforts to rally broad electoral coalitions that lack these shared understandings. We therefore contend that the level of collective identities represents a good place to study the interaction between structure and agency. While our evidence demonstrates that group identities remain anchored in social structure, they are clearly closer to the discourses of political actors than identities defined by class or education, which are rarely referred to directly in contemporary political discourse.

While our theoretical perspective and the findings so far lead us to anticipate some basic similarities between countries in terms of the group identities underlying the universalism–particularism divide, substantial differences in timing when it comes to the crystallization of the new cleavage should become visible in identity-to-politics linkages. Such country differences should be more pronounced for the Far Right than for the New Left block. The mobilization of the New Left pole dates back to the 1980s and 1990s (Inglehart 1984; Kitschelt 1994; Kriesi 1998), and should by now be consolidated. In this respect, it is of minor importance for the social rootedness of the new cleavage whether the core support groups of the New Left pole are aligned with transformed Social Democratic, Socialist, or Green parties – or whether they switch between parties within the same block. By focusing on party blocks, rather than individual parties, we are able to filter out quite a lot of noise deriving, among other factors, from institutional differences (Wlezien and Jennings 2023). Substantially more variance should be visible due to differences in the timing of the rise of the Far Right. While the French Front National (now Rassemblement National) and the Swiss People's Party already gained substantial vote shares in the 1980s and the 1990s, respectively, parties of a similar type only emerged much more recently in Germany and Britain.

4.2 How Identities Shape Voter Alignments with Ideological Blocks

We start out by considering to which extent the new group identities we focus on have been mobilized in our four countries. Figure 10 shows how voters of the three party blocks deviate from the country averages in their feelings of closeness to four groups that most clearly and distinctively separate voters of the New Left (white bars) from voters of the Far Right (black bars). Positive deviations from the country mean indicate that voters feel closer to this group and negative deviations indicate the opposite. We chose to focus here on the most important group identities associated with the new cleavage: cosmopolitans, down-to-earth people, conationals, and people with a migration background. The results for all seventeen groups that we measured can be found in the online appendix.

The most striking finding conveyed in Figure 10 is that the politicization of group antagonisms is extremely similar across contexts. In each of the four countries, those who lean toward the Far Right identify strongly with their nationality and feel particularly close to "people who are down-to-earth and rooted to home." That said, in France, the UK, and in Germany, the mainstream Right also mobilizes successfully among these groups. While there is evidence for some degree of competition between the Far Right and the mainstream

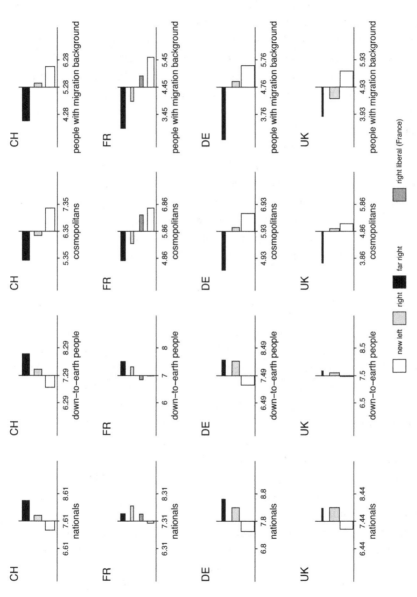

Figure 10 Identity divergence between supporters of party blocks, new group identities

Right, the Far Right and the New Left clearly constitute the antagonists along the new divide. Throughout our four countries, the parties of the New Left draw disproportionate support from people identifying as cosmopolitans and those who feel close to people with migration backgrounds. In terms of their group identities, the voters of the New Left and Far Right party families constitute the mirror images of each other: The in-group of one electorate constitutes the out-group of the other. This pattern is most pronounced for the in-groups of the New Left, namely, cosmopolitans and people with a migration background.

The case of France is complicated by the breakthrough of Emmanuel Macron as an exponent of the Right-Liberal block (see Section 2), who has split the Left voter block (Gougou and Persico 2017). Overall, those supporting Macron's coalition align with the voters of the New Left in terms of their group identities, although the universalist penchant of this electorate is more ambiguous.

The height of the individual bars is proportional to the size of the electoral bloc in the respective country. While the electorates of the New Left, the Right, and the Far Right in the four cases do not differ fundamentally in the groups they feel close to, the relative strength of the party blocks at the poles of the new divide differs a lot more. Indeed, the Far Right is substantially stronger in Switzerland and France than in Germany or the UK, where realignment has played out much more recently. We interpret the overall results as a sign of the potential for an equally fully realigned preference space in the UK and in Germany. Furthermore, it is striking to see that rising vote shares among the Far Right do not dilute the (self-)perceptions of its voters. Even though Far Right parties in France and Switzerland have succeeded in rallying much larger swaths of the electorate, their voters' identities diverge just as massively and starkly from the New Left as in countries where the Far Right is still confined to the fringes of the party system.

How strong are these divisions compared to objective group categories that are considered important bases of contemporary alignments? Figure 11 shows the results for identification with people with higher education and rural residents, two categories that a large literature has identified as underlying alignments in contemporary politics (see Sections 1 and 2). We start with education, the most powerful objective basis of the new universalism–particularism cleavage according to the literature. Indeed, Far Right voters stand out as feeling particularly distant from the highly educated.[14] The fact that those feeling close

---

[14] This is consistent with the finding of Abrassart and Wolter (2023), according to which the voters of the Radical Right assign less importance to education as a basis of prestige.

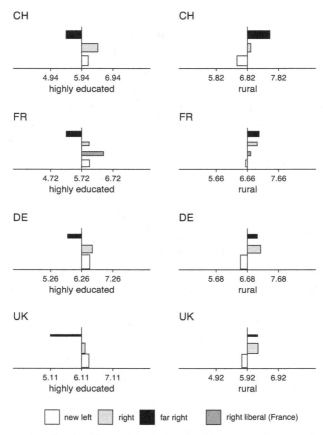

Figure 11 Identity divergence between supporters of party blocks, objective groups

to this group are found both in the electorate of the New Left and established Right (while they are overrepresented among the Right Liberal block in France) reflects the well-known split within the middle class, parts of which lean to the left, while others have remained loyal to the Right (Kriesi 1998, Kitschelt and Rehm 2014). While those with higher education constitute an out-group for Far Right voters, the latter do not feel particularly close to people with low or intermediate levels of education, which constitute their voter base in objective terms (e.g., Bornschier and Kriesi 2013; see full results in the online-appendix). This reflects the tendency we highlighted for individuals to seek identification with positively connoted groups.

One such group amenable to positive identification might be "rural people." While constituting a structural category, individuals may identify to varying degrees as rural even if they live in suburban contexts or small towns. While rural sentiment appears less structured by party preference than was the case for the culturally connoted group identities, we see that rural sentiment is strongest among the voters of the Far Right in Switzerland and France as the early realigning cases, with the effect standing out as particularly strong in the former case. In Germany and the UK, rural identity remains somewhat stronger among mainstream Right than for Far Right voters. Rural inhabitants do not constitute a consistent out-group for New Left voters, on the other hand.

What about the importance of older group identities which have their roots in the traditional state market and religious cleavages? Figure 12 shows the results for two identities associated with the traditional cleavages (closeness to "wealthy people" and those with "Christian-Western values," respectively). The first thing to notice is that the mirror image to those voting for the New Left are now those supporting the mainstream Right, rather than the Far Right. Reminiscent of the historically strong religious cleavages, voters of the traditional Right feel close to people "with Christian-Western values." Moreover, mainstream Right voters, or, in the case of France, those making up Macron's coalition, feel closer to the wealthy. Although the antagonism seems to have weakened, closeness to people "with Christian-Western values" continues to reflect the religious cleavage with the New Left constituting the secular and the mainstream Right the religious pole of the cleavage. These categories do not seem to form part of the collective identity foundation of the universalism–particularism cleavage.[15]

Overall, these results suggest that group identities correlate strongly with alignments along the three ideological blocks. In the appendix to this section, we move to a multivariate setting in which we gauge the effect of the most salient identities on vote choice, controlling for social structural variables. For each electorate, we identify the three most distinctive in-groups and out-groups and include them in a multivariate regression model. The results confirm those presented in this section and underline the substantive importance of the group identities we focus on for vote choice. The analysis of the three most relevant in-groups and out-groups also impressively confirms the symmetric antagonism between the New Left and the Far Right: in particular, the key in-groups of the New Left ("feminists," "people with a migration background," "cosmopolitans") are precisely the key out-groups of Far Right voters.

---

[15] While the Far Right's discourse of defending the Christian heritage would seem to suggest an affinity of those feeling close to Christian-Western values to the Far Right, Pless, Tromp, and Houtman (2023) show that religious and secular value divides are distinct in Western Europe.

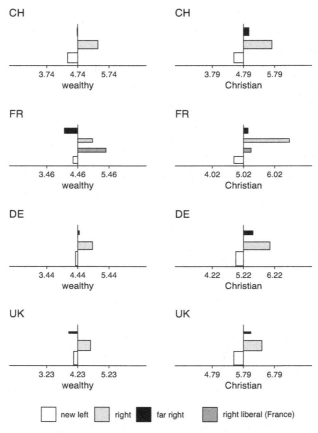

Figure 12 Identity divergence between supporters of party blocks, old structural group identities

To summarize the analysis so far in substantive terms, we find that with the exception of the rejection of the higher educated by Far Right voters, economically connoted identity groups (pertaining to education, vertical class, people with humble financial means, as shown in the appendix) divide the self-perceptions of voters much less than more culturally connoted identity groups. It is also important to notice that social structuration and politicization of group identities are not identical. Comparing the results presented here to those in Section 3, we observe that some of the group identities that are highly structured by objective social position (such as education, wealth, and income) are not clearly divisive between political camps. Reversely, the divisive potential of "cosmopolitans" is clearly stronger and more explicit than that exhibited by education groups or social classes.

4.3 An Overarching Group Antagonism Underlying the New Cleavage?

In the preceding analyses, we have looked at group identities separately. But it is obvious that some group identifications are likely to overlap, while others are antagonistically related. To what extent do various identities cluster into a more overarching antagonism? To address this question, we perform a discriminant analysis that seeks to determine which combination of group identities most powerfully predicts vote choice for the New Left, Right, and Far Right party blocks. We leave out the French Right Liberals here because their inclusion invariably results in an additional dimension setting apart this group of voters from all others, which is due to the rather unique composition of this electorate that we documented in the prior analyses.

The discriminant analysis based on all seventeen group identities included in our survey yields two dimensions and is reported in Table 3. The first function is very powerful in terms of the canonical correlation, highly significant, and explains most of the variance. Shaped by closeness to feminists, people with migration background and conationals, cosmopolitans, and culturally interested people, it is closely related to the universalism–particularism dimension and strongly discriminates the voters of the New Left and the Far Right. Beyond the frequently invoked importance of the immigration issue for understanding the emergence of the Far Right, this suggests that the underlying backlash is broader, and extends to issues such as gender equality (Off 2023), transnationalism (Hooghe and Marks 2018), and universalistic values more generally. The group means on the canonical variables indicate that New Left voters are situated at one pole and Far Right voters at the opposing pole of this dimension, while mainstream Right voters lie in between.

While closeness to people working in the social and educational sector is also to some extent associated with this first dimension, this is hardly the case for the other groups defined by income and education. Urban-rural identities are not particularly prominent in shaping the overarching identity antagonism that divides New Left and Far Right voters either, even if the direction of their association with the overarching divide is as expected. The group identities that stand out as most unique for the two political camps, however, are clearly those that have been central to the way that the New Left and the Far Right have framed conflicts over identity.

The second function is interesting in that it sheds light on what distinguishes voters of the traditional Right from their Far Right counterparts. While substantially weaker in statistical terms and in the variance explained,

Table 3 Linear canonical discriminant analysis of seventeen group identities as predictors of voting for the New Left, Right, and Far Right party blocks

Group identities	Canonical structure	
	Function 1	**Function 2**
Education		
Higher education degree	0.19	**0.46**
Intermediate education	−0.12	−0.07
Lower-level education	−0.02	−0.23
Income and occupation		
Wealthy people	−0.15	**0.44**
Humble economic means	0.04	**−0.36**
Hard working	−0.20	−0.10
Creative work	0.15	−0.02
Work in social and educational sector	**0.35**	0.16
Residence		
Rural people	−0.28	−0.14
Urban people	0.23	0.24
Political and belonging		
Feminists	**0.59**	−0.15
Migration background	**0.56**	**0.37**
Cosmopolitans	**0.38**	0.21
Culturally interested	**0.32**	0.15
Down-to-earth	−0.27	0.00
Conationals	**−0.36**	0.10
Religious		
Christian-Western values	−0.21	**0.63**
N	9957	
Canonical correlation	0.48	0.24
Eigenvalue	0.30	0.06
Prop. variance explained	83 percent	17 percent
p-value of F-statistic	0.000	0.000
Group means on canonical variables		
New Left	0.54	−0.07
Right	−0.35	0.32
Far Right	−0.81	−0.37

Note: Loadings equal to or above 0.30 are set in bold.

the function is substantially very meaningful. Two types of identity stand out, one of them related to the religious and the other to the economic cleavage. Whereas Christian-Western values are important in the self-definition of traditional Right voters, this is not the case for those of the Far Right. This indicates that the remains of the religious cleavage mitigate Far Right voting. In terms of education and income, the analysis reveals an interesting vertical rift between the mainstream Right and the Far Right: Those voting for the mainstream Right feel closer to wealthy people and to those with higher education, and to some extent more remote from individuals with humble economic means. There is also a difference in terms of identifying with people with migration background indicating that the divide within the right-wing spectrum is not solely related to vertical social status.

Overall, the group identities included in the model correctly predict vote choice for 63 percent of the respondents who declared they would cast their ballot for a party belonging to the New Left block. The prediction for Far Right voters is similarly powerful (roughly 59 percent of respondents are correctly classified). Not surprisingly, given the importance of the first function on which mainstream Right voters occupy an intermediate position, these group identities are somewhat less predictive of the mainstream Right vote, but still help explain the vote choice of almost half of the mainstream Right respondents. These figures call into question stark formulations of the dealignment hypothesis, suggesting instead that partisan alignments remain to a considerable degree structured by group identities.

As we set out in Section 1, the underlying structure in electoral behavior becomes visible if we look at party competition from the perspective of group identities and if we consider vote choice for ideologically defined party blocks. This final part of the empirical analysis presented in this section further substantiates our claim that much of the instability of fragmentation witnessed in recent decades stems from competition *within* the New Left, Liberal, Right, and Far Right party blocks.

4.4 Discussion

The results presented in this section reveal a high degree of similarity in the mobilization of the universalism–particularism cleavage across contexts. We posit that these similarities are visible only if we study voter alignments at a higher level of abstraction, which involves two steps.

The first is to incorporate *group identities as mediators* between social structural position and partisan alignments. We showed in Section 3 that group identities are rooted in social structure. This introduces an element of inertia despite more volatile political landscapes. This first factor instills more stability over time and a higher degree of similarity across contexts than is acknowledged in accounts that put key emphasis on political agency. We also showed that as parties link broad identity potentials to the political manifestation of the universalism–particularism cleavage, these group identifications are aggregated into higher-order identities that have a stronger political flavor.

Second, we have demonstrated that taking *party blocks* – rather than individual parties – as units of analysis filters out quite a lot of noise in terms of political behavior. Indeed, while electoral behavior may have become more volatile, it remains strongly constrained by voters' broader allegiances, as our analysis of party affinities across and within blocks revealed. Taking the distinction between the New Left, Right, and Far Right as our unit of analysis, we show that party blocks differ fundamentally in terms of their central in-groups and out-groups. The multivariate analyses provided in the online appendix underscore that, controlling for voters' social structural characteristics, their central in-groups and out-groups are massively important predictors of vote choice.

When it comes to the role of political agency, it is interesting to note that our findings (see Table A4.1 in the appendix for details) reveal both important symmetries and an element of asymmetry in the antagonism between the New Left and the Far Right. On the one hand, it is striking that the in-groups of the New Left – "feminists," "people with migration background," and "cosmopolitans" – constitute the core out-groups of the Far Right. This testifies to our claim that the universalism–particularism divide has become a full-blown cleavage that is rooted in structural potentials transcending specific country contexts. On the other hand, the in-groups of the Far Right are more diverse across contexts, underscoring the reactive nature of the rise of this party family, and hence the more important role of agency at the Far Right end of the cleavage.

The most important reflection of political agency lies, however, in the relative strength of party blocks across contexts. While the Far Right rallies roughly a third of the electorate in presidential elections in France and in parliamentary elections in Switzerland, it is far weaker in Germany and the UK, where the established parties have until recently been rather successful in absorbing the anti-universalistic and particularistic potential. And yet, the similarities in the links between group identities and party blocks in our set of four countries again suggest that these links are rooted in processes of social closure that are partly pre-political. We take our results to reflect different stages of the realignment process along the universalism–particularism cleavage, which the next section will further delve into. While our analysis mainly focused on the cleavage between the New Left and the Far Right, we found that voters of the mainstream Right also have distinctive affinities. The fact that identities related to class and religion are still present speaks to the cleavage approach and to the idea of a "layering" of historical conflicts (Off 2023).

With that said, mainstream Right voters do tend to identify with some of the same cultural identity groups that Far Right voters feel particularly close or distant to (e.g., demarcation from feminists, from people with migration background, and national identity). At the same time, a vertical status divide exists between the two blocks on the right, mirrored in differential affinities to the wealthy and the highly educated, speaking to ongoing realignment between the mainstream Right and the Far Right (e.g., Gidron and Ziblatt 2019). The case of Macron's "République en Marche" fuses elements of the New Left–Far Right divide and the divide between the mainstream Right and the Far Right into one. The individual case can be explained by institutional specificities of French politics and Macron's trajectory from a socialist to a more fiscally conservative stance. In terms of our theory, it will be relevant to see if "after Macron" the main divide revolves back to a New Left versus Far Right one, or whether the particular pro-welfare stance of the Rassemblement National will stabilize a cleavage that sidelines the New Left.

5 Parties as Representatives of Social Identities

The previous sections demonstrated, first, how emerging identity antagonisms are rooted in social structure and, second, how they divide the electorates of the New Left and the Far Right. This final empirical section takes us closer to the political element of a crystallizing cleavage: It focuses on political parties as crucial links between processes of social closure and the political realm. It also shifts attention from the cross-country commonalities to the variation in how, when, and by whom identity potentials ultimately become mobilized. From looking at broader party blocks that reveal cross-national patterns in politicized identity divides, we move to a focus on individual parties and zoom in on specific country comparisons. In doing so, we are necessarily selective. Hence, we focus on those comparisons that we find to be most instructive.

Our primary empirical interest here is in how voters associate parties with identity groups. In other words, we want to know how perceptions of group belonging tie in with people's mental maps of the party system. Research on electoral realignment has traced objectively shifting links between parties and groups, but *voters' perceptions* of new alignments can be taken as a measure of how fundamentally, lastingly, perhaps irreversibly party systems have changed. Are the Social Democrats perceived as the party of "hard-working people," or is this group's representation attributed to the Far Right? To what extent have left-wing parties become associated with urban, cosmopolitan, or highly educated groups in the eyes of voters? If the coordinates of the party system have truly realigned along a new cleavage, respondents, including those who do not identify with a group themselves, should consistently link universalist-particularist groups to the corresponding political parties. This perception should be clearer where the development of the cleavage is advanced and consolidated. An analogy would be that at the height of the class cleavage, workers, nonworkers, pensioners, and self-employed would consistently associate the working class with socialist parties.

To study to what extent this is the case for the universalism–particularism cleavage, we asked respondents to link social groups to specific political parties. Our results based on these associations support the notion of an organizational dimension of cleavage formation. Most fundamentally, we find that voters have a pretty accurate mental map of their countries' party system. The associations that we uncovered in the preceding section between group belonging and political alignments indeed shape many voters' understanding of their national party systems.

Compared to the rest of the sections, this section more strongly emphasizes the *cross-country dimension*. We focus on a comparison between Germany and Switzerland. These countries are most comparable in terms of their electoral system and with regard their party systems. In particular, both countries still have important mainstream left and mainstream right parties. However, they differ on one crucial dimension that is the focus of our interest: Whereas Switzerland saw an early political realignment along a universalism–particularism cleavage (similar to France), this cleavage was only politicized more recently in Germany (like in the UK). This is a crucial difference that allows us to study whether party strategies affect how similar structural conditions are being translated into political outcomes.

Focusing on this comparison, we first show that voters in early-realigned Switzerland have more congealed perceptions of the transformed links between identity groups and party blocks than voters in late-realigned Germany. Swiss voters associate the working class with the Far Right and the "cosmopolitan" middle class with the New Left. This is less clearly the case in Germany.

Second, looking at *cohort differences* reveals that group–party links are more aligned with the new cleavage for younger voters, while older voters are more likely to think about group–party links along the cleavage structures of the twentieth century (especially in terms of class). This is observable in Germany as well as in Switzerland, albeit starting from different baselines.

Third, we see that perceived voter–group ties in these countries also reflect the *specific* ways that parties have positioned themselves with respect to a newly emerging cleavage over the years. This is most evident for the Social Democrats. Indeed, it is here that the distinction between party blocks and individual parties becomes highly relevant. The Swiss Social Democrats established themselves as the representative of a new middle class early on, in step with a newly emerging Green party (Häusermann et al. 2022). By contrast, the German SPD kept its status as the main representative of the working class, including in the eyes of voters. At the same time, the SPD never became the main representative of the new urban, educated, and cosmopolitan middle class. Instead, this role was taken by the Greens, who are today much more firmly linked to "universalist" identity groups in German voters' perceptions.

5.1 Perceived Voter–Party Links from a Cleavage Perspective

At the center of this section is the question of how cleavages are organized. The traditional cleavage literature emphasized the role of organizations such as trade unions, churches, and associations. However, these organizations have seen massive declines in membership and political influence over recent decades (Gingrich and Lynch 2019). While social movements may have partly replaced them, cleavages are also organized by parties themselves. For example, a recently growing literature demonstrates how parties use group-based appeals to attract the votes of specific social groups (Thau 2019; Thau 2021; Huber 2022; Mierke-Zatwarnicki 2022). Parties do not just target identities related to traditional cleavages – for example, by appealing to people's class – but also those related to new or reemerging lines of social conflict, such as voters' education, geographical residence, or other important group memberships (Huber 2022; Dolinsky 2023).

While these studies ask about the behavior of parties, we focus on the perceptions of voters:[16] How do voters understand the alignment of social groups and political parties? Do these perceptions reflect the processes of cleavage formation that we studied in the preceding sections?

So far, the question of what people think/know about party–voter links has mainly been studied in the US. The importance of voters' perception of group–party links is demonstrated by Kane, Mason, and Wronski (2021), who find that

---

[16] A recent experimental literature also studies the effects of group-based appeals, for example, Robison et al. (2021), Jacobs and Munis (2019); Dassonneville, Stubager, and Thau (2022).

the link between a voter's own group membership and his or her party identification is moderated by the knowledge of other group members' party identification. This moderation, however, presupposes that people know how members of different social groups vote. Hence, the literature has started to study people's perception of group–party alignments. Goggin, Henderson, and Theodoridis (2020) find that people are quite good at inferring a candidate's party when given information about the candidate's policy positions. In a study on the UK, Titelman and Lauderdale (2023) demonstrate that people can infer voting behavior from demographic characteristics of voters. At the same time, voters suffer from a substantive base rate fallacy and overestimate the role of small but highly visible elements of a party's voter coalition. In particular, voters overestimate the share of out-group members in the out-party's support base (e.g., Republicans heavily overestimate the share of LGBT in the Democratic voter base) (Ahler and Sood 2018).

In two-party systems, linking social groups to political parties is relatively straightforward, whereas it is considerably more difficult in multiparty systems. Accordingly, most of the existing literature on multiparty systems focuses on parties' left-right positioning (Busch 2016; Meyer and Wagner 2020; Nasr 2020). In work that has a stronger focus on the perception of group members' political behavior, Sczepanski (2022) shows that voters in Austria and Italy have relatively clear perceptions of which group would support leaving the European Union – which is, however, again a binary decision.

Building on these results, this section focuses on three aspects of people's perceptions of group–party links: (i) people's mental maps in terms of broader ideological blocks, (ii) generational differences in these broader perceptions, and (iii) perceived links between specific parties and groups within an ideological block (the New Left, in this case).

First, we ask to what extent voters also have an accurate mental map of the party system in multiparty contexts. Our general theoretical argument suggests that voters should be quite able to predict the voting behavior of specific social groups. After all, if we observe the formation of a new cleavage, voters should increasingly understand politics through this lens. We thus expect that those identities that strongly characterize the universalist pole of the cleavage are clearly associated with left parties. By contrast, those identities that most strongly characterize the particularistic pole should be associated with Far Right parties. At the same time, we expect important differences between our examples of early and late realignment. Cross-country variation in the assignment of groups to specific party blocks should be structured by the timing of realignment and the emergence of new parties. In cases of early realignment, left-wing parties clearly positioned themselves at the universalistic pole of the cleavage. In addition, early successes of the Far Right further fueled the mobilization and polarization of the universalist–particularist divide. This meant that the Left faced increasing competition in the representation of many relatively lower-status groups today associated with the particularistic pole. In cases of late realignment, left parties have remained more likely to be seen as representatives of lower class groups.

In addition, there are potential differences in the demarcation between mainstream Right and Far Right. Again, in cases of early realignment, the rise of the Far Right meant that these parties came to be seen as the main representative of key groups at the particularistic pole of the new cleavage (such as native nationals, rural dwellers, defenders of traditional conservative values). In cases of late realignment (where opportunity structures, mainstream party strategies, institutional hurdles, and so on obstructed Far Right party entry), the lack of a new party at this pole meant that the mainstream Right was able to compete for this position much longer (often building on nationalist or conservative legacies). They potentially even absorbed part of an increasingly activated nativist-nationalist Far Right electoral potential while left-wing parties started to cater to segments of a growing (progressive, urban) new middle class.

In the second step of our analysis, and still operating with broader ideological blocks, we explore the role of cohorts. The new cleavage structure should be clearer and more crystallized in the perception of younger voters than in the perception of older voters, who originally internalized a more traditional cleavage structure. Therefore, their perception of party system alignments should still partly be structured by more traditional divides.

In the third and final step of our analysis, we zoom into the left block and onto the contrast between the Greens and the Social Democrats.[17] Here, we not only look at the perception of parties as such but also at its relationship with vote choice. In principle, it is irrelevant for cleavage formation which specific parties within broader ideological blocks are at the forefront of mobilizing newly emerging electoral potentials. However, we would expect voters' perceptions of group–party ties to reflect the specificities of parties' mobilization histories,

---

[17] We could do the same within the mainstream right block, where there is also variation in how exactly specific parties reacted and/or contributed to the mobilization of a nativist-nationalist electoral potential. However, contrasting the former political arm of the working-class movement, the Social Democrats, with the Greens, shows nicely how historically determined categorizations into party families are less helpful for understanding parties' role in contemporary cleavage formation.

which are conditioned by context factors but also result from strategic decisions over how to react to structural change, newly arising issues, or emerging competitors. Arguably, for no party family has the discussion of trade-offs presented by a transforming social and political landscape been as prominent as for the Social Democrats (Häusermann and Kitschelt 2024). Social Democrats in cases of early realignment had the opportunity to politically mobilize the new cleavage early on, giving them a good chance to become the representatives of universalist groups in the eyes of voters. In cases of later realignment, by contrast, the Social Democrats were able to ignore or blur their positions on a new cleavage for longer. Where the Social Democrats did *not* claim representation of "universalist" groups, the Greens are more likely to be seen today as the main party representing the progressive end of the cleavage.

5.2 Mental Maps of Ideological Blocks, across Cohorts, and for Specific Parties

The question that we use in the following analyses presented respondents with the familiar battery of seventeen social groups and asked them about their perception of group members' voting behavior. To learn about people's perception of group–party links, we asked the following question: "Which party would you associate most closely with each of the following groups? In other words, which party do you think the members of each group would be most likely to vote for?"

We presented respondents with a choice of the six major parties in each country as well as with a "don't know" option. This question deliberately combines two somewhat different logics: The second part of the question refers to an objective likelihood that should be influenced by the base rate – for most social groups, the relative majority of their members will vote for a country's biggest party. By contrast, the first part of the question asks for a more subject-ive evaluation of the association between groups and parties that allows people to link smaller parties to certain groups. While these dimensions of the question may objectively point into slightly different directions, they allow respondents to take the complexity of multiparty systems into account.

In the presentation of the results, we start by grouping parties in our ideo-logical blocks (the New Left, the mainstream Right, and the Far Right), before we then move to the party level. We show results for the four key identities that most clearly tap into different aspects typically associated with a universalistic–particularistic cleavage (as shown in the preceding sections). Moreover, we add two more identities to better explore the demarcation between the Left and Far Right ("people who do hard, tiring work") and between mainstream Right and Far Right ("rural people").

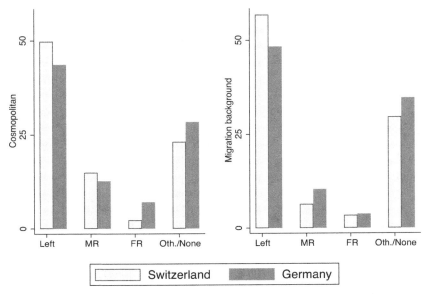

Figure 13 Perception of group–party associations, universalistic
identities

5.2.1 Ideological Blocks

Our first aim is to understand how accurate voters' mental map of their
national party systems is: Do voters perceive the same links between identities
and party blocks that emerged from our analysis in Section 4? We start with
the universalistic identities: cosmopolitans and people with migration background. As Figure 13 shows, both identities are strongly associated with
parties on the left, in line with our previous findings.[18] This holds both in
Germany and in Switzerland, and reflects the fact that both countries saw an
early transformation of the Left, most evident in the emergence of Green
parties.

Next, we move to the key particularistic identities, conationals, and people
who are "down-to-earth and rooted to home." Here, Figure 14 shows
a somewhat more nuanced picture. In Germany, both identities are clearly
associated with the mainstream Right. Down-to-earth people are even somewhat associated with the Left. In Switzerland, by contrast, both identities are
associated with the Far Right. Going back to Figure 10 in the previous section,

---

[18] As in the previous analyses, the Swiss bars for mainstream right parties add the FDP and the
CVP/Mitte. The "other/none" bar only contains respondents that explicitly picked this option.
For ease of presentation, those who picked Die Linke or FDP in Germany or GLP in Switzerland
are not included in this graph.

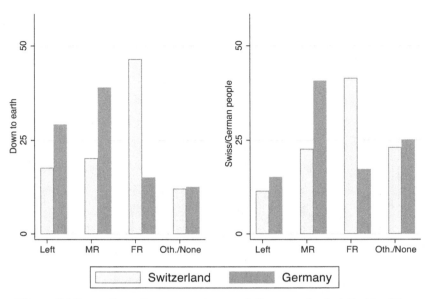

Figure 14 Perception of group–party associations, particularistic identities

we see that the perception of Swiss voters closely corresponds to actual voting behavior. In Germany, both identities are almost equally strongly associated with voting for the mainstream Right and for the Far Right. In a direct comparison with Switzerland, it thus seems accurate that these identities are also more strongly associated with the mainstream Right by voters themselves.

Finally, in Figure 15, we look at the more traditional identities, "people who do hard, tiring work" and rural people, for which we expect political associations to have shifted compared to a Lipset–Rokkanian world. For "rural," we find the same pattern as for the particularistic identities: It is associated with the mainstream Right (and partly with the Left) in Germany and with the Far Right in Switzerland.[19] Interestingly, "Hard, tiring work" is associated with the Left in Germany but with the Far Right in Switzerland. A close look at the data used in Section 4 shows that these perceptions are again very accurate for Switzerland, in the sense that they match how identification relates to vote choice. In Germany, by contrast, both identities are only weakly correlated with political behavior. Interestingly, these perceived voter–block links are almost identical

---

[19] In other words, the formerly agrarian far right party in Switzerland has managed to keep "ownership" of this identity even as it massively expanded its voter base beyond rural areas. This reflects the stickiness of old cleavage identities as well as party's ability to associate them with newer forms of group conflict (Zollinger 2023).

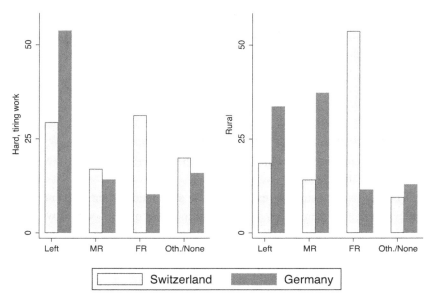

Figure 15 Perception of group–party associations, contested identities

for those who strongly identify and those who do not identify at all with a group themselves (see appendix Figures A5.1–A5.6).

Ultimately, these three graphs support our main contention that voters have a relatively accurate mental map of group–party links on the level of ideological blocks. They consistently identify the block whose voters most strongly identify with a social group as the main representative of that social group. Moreover, telling differences between Germany and Switzerland emerge. At the universalistic pole, associations between groups and parties are very similar in both countries. At the particularistic pole, however, down-to-earth, Swiss, and rural people are all predominantly associated with the Far Right SVP in Switzerland. In Germany, by contrast, these identities are (still) clearly associated with the mainstream Right. Finally, people "who do hard, tiring work" are still associated with the traditional class cleavage (and thus with the Left) in Germany. At almost 50 percent, this is the strongest association we see with any German party block across all six identities. In Switzerland, the picture is very different. Here, the same group is associated with the new cleavage and the Far Right in particular. The realignment of the traditional working class seems largely complete in the eyes of Swiss voters. This suggests that the timing and intensity of realignment also affects voters' perceptions of the party system.

In Figures A5.7–A5.9 in the appendix, we show the same graphs for France and England. Here, the character of a two-party system comes out very clearly in the UK. Not only cosmopolitanism and a migration background are clearly associated with the left but also down-to-earth and hard work. This points to the weakness of the Far Right, as well as to the persisting upper class connotation of the mainstream right. Whereas rural is associated to an equal extent with the left and the mainstream right, conationals is the only category that is associated to a substantial degree with the Far Right (although less than with the mainstream right). Other research indicates that given the constraints of the British party system, Brexit might be more tightly linked to the political articulation of a new cleavage than partisanship, which cross-cuts the Leave/Remain camps (Hobolt, Leeper, and Tilley 2021).

In France, we see stronger evidence of an association of the particularistic pole with the Far Right. Here, nationals are most strongly associated with the Far Right, which also scores relatively highly on rural, down-to-earth, and hard work. However, the association of hard work with the left is even stronger, thanks to the reinvigoration of the state–market cleavage by Mélenchon's France Insoumise (the more detailed results show that it is this party, rather than the other components of the left, that voters associate with the hard working). This suggests that the relative strength of cleavage dimensions matters for the realigning potential of the new cleavage: Where the economic dimension remains polarized, the left and the Far Right may compete for some of the same voters. In this sense, France is more similar to Germany, where the Social Democrats were able to retain voters harboring these identities due to their reluctance to fully embrace a New Left position, than to Switzerland. Consistent with the three other cases, cosmopolitanism and migration background are clearly associated with the New Left block in France.[20]

5.2.2 Cohort Differences

In the next step of the analysis, we look at cohort differences in the perception of parties. Here, our hypothesis is that the mental map of younger voters, who have been politically socialized after the transition to the knowledge economy and the politicization of new issues, should reflect the new cleavage in more crystallized ways than the mental map of older voters. This difference should most strongly concern those identities which always mattered to politics but in which there has been a shift in who represents them, such as hard-working or conational. By contrast, we would expect weaker differences for identities such as "cosmopolitan," since older people probably did not develop a strong

---

[20] Although Jean-Luc Mélenchon's embrace of universalism is disputed, Gougou and Persico (2017) show that the voters of his La France Insoumise are clearly situated in the left-universalist quadrant, conforming to the elite-level analysis in Section 2.

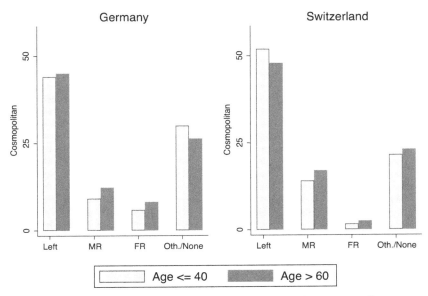

Figure 16 Perception of group–party associations for cosmopolitans, two age groups

political image of these identities in their youth, that is, before these groups were strongly politicized.

Indeed, when looking at the assignment of "cosmopolitan people," we hardly see any differences between respondents under the age of forty and respondents over the age of sixty (Figure 16). This is quite different, however, for people "doing hard, tiring work" (Figure 17). Here, the oldest respondents in both countries still seem to see the party system through the traditional class-cleavage structure. This is much less the case for younger respondents. In Germany, a plurality still associates people doing hard, tiring work with the Left (i.e., with Social Democrats), but the share is much lower for younger than for older voters. In Switzerland, a plurality of younger respondents even associates this group with the Far Right. Similarly, there is a substantial age difference for conationals. Among the elderly in both countries, this identity is more strongly associated with the mainstream right than among younger voters (Figure 18).

Of the other three identities of interest, the pattern for people with "migration background" is very similar to the pattern for "cosmopolitans." There is a somewhat higher share of "don't knows" among the old, but the relative order of the parties is the same across age groups. Similarly, the pattern for "down-to-earth" is very similar to the pattern for conationals (see appendix, Figures A5.10 and A5.11). The only identity where age plays a role in one

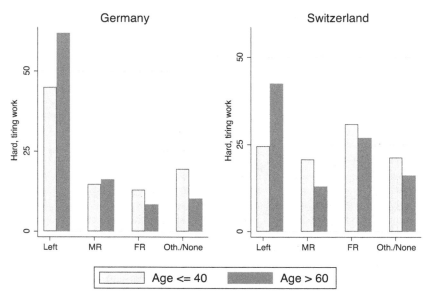

Figure 17 Perception of group–party associations for people who do hard work, two age groups

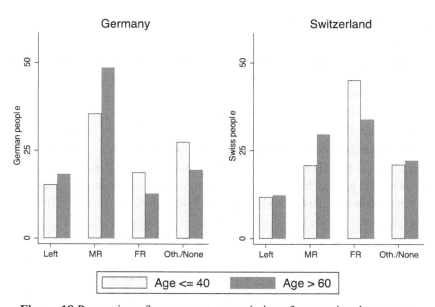

Figure 18 Perception of group–party associations for conationals, two age groups

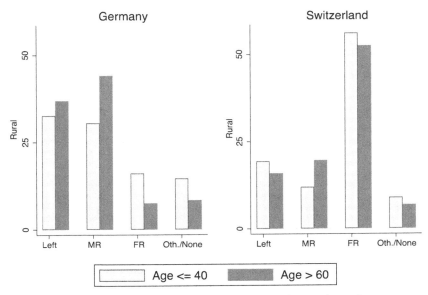

Figure 19 Perception of group–party associations for rural people, two age groups

country but not in the other is "rural" (Figure 19). Here, Germany shows the familiar pattern of a stronger alignment with the new cleavage among the young than among the old. This is not the case in Switzerland, where majorities of all age groups associate "rural" with the SVP. This reflects the fact that the SVP used to be a farmer's party before it developed into a Far Right party.

5.2.3 Differences within the Left Block

We now move on from looking at blocks to the level of individual parties. Since there is only one Far Right party in both countries, and since the demarcation between FDP and CVP in Switzerland is of less theoretical interest in the context of the new cleavage, we focus on the demarcation within the left block regarding the universalistic identities. For Switzerland, this means that we compare the Social Democrats and the Greens. In Germany, we add Die Linke as a third party within the left bloc.

As Figures 20 and 21 show, there are considerable differences between both countries. In Switzerland, cosmopolitans and people with a migration background are more strongly associated with the Social Democrats than with the Greens. In Germany, both identities are much more strongly associated with the Greens.

Regarding people "who do hard, tiring work," we had already seen that this identity is clearly associated with the Far Right in Switzerland and more with

European Politics

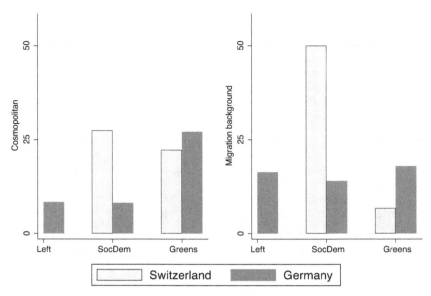

Figure 20 Perception of group–party associations on the left, universalistic identities

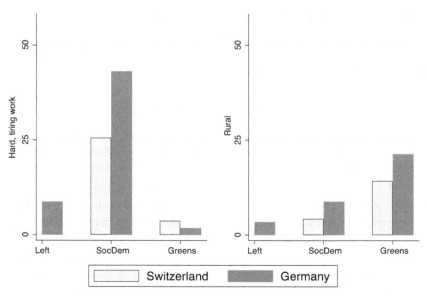

Figure 21 Perception of group–party associations on the left, contested identities

the Left in Germany. Figure 21 now reveals that this pattern is mainly driven by the Social Democrats, and, to some extent, by Die Linke. This confirms that we really observe a more traditional perception of cleavages here: This group is not at all associated with the New Left (the Greens) but with the more traditional Social Democratic or even post-Communist Left. Rural, finally, is an identity where we don't see strong differences between the two countries.

To some extent, these differences are likely due to differences in the baseline of party sizes. The Swiss Social Democrats are roughly twice as strong as the Greens, while the German Greens and Social Democrats roughly performed on the same level in many recent (state-level and European) elections. This makes it much more likely a priori that a "typical" universalist voter in Switzerland votes for the Social Democrats. Nevertheless, these effects are much stronger than what could be explained by pure baseline effects.

To further explore this within-block variation, we now connect perceptions of the party system with individual vote choices. In Section 4, we demonstrated that identities are systematically associated with the choice of different party blocks. Here, we now further differentiate this relationship within the left block.

5.2.4 Relationship with Vote Choice

Figures 22 demonstrates the association between closeness to cosmopolitans/ hard-working people and support for Social Democrats/Greens. Both figures

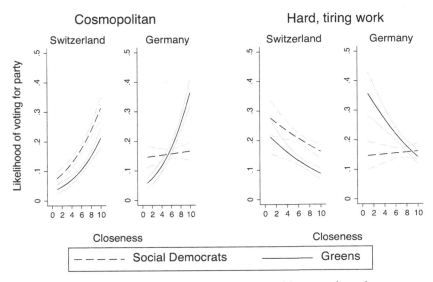

Figure 22 Closeness to cosmopolitans/hard-working people and support for left parties

further demonstrate striking differences between Germany and Switzerland. In Switzerland, identifying as a cosmopolitan is almost equally strongly correlated with voting for the Social Democrats and with voting for the Greens. In Germany, by contrast, this identity only correlates with support for the Greens, while there is no correlation at all with voting Social Democrat.

The right-hand part of the figure shows the reverse picture for people doing hard, tiring work. In Switzerland, this identity is negatively correlated with voting for both left parties. In Germany, by contrast, it is not correlated with the Social Democrats but negatively with the Greens.

Thus, we again see cross-country differences that are in line with our argument about the role of early and late realignment and the Swiss Social Democrats' comparatively early adoption of a New Left platform. In Switzerland, universalism is significantly associated with support for the Social Democrats. In Germany, by contrast, the prototypical universalistic identities, cosmopolitanism, and migration background are not significantly related with voting for the Social Democrats. The profile of the Greens is much more similar in both countries. While the prototypical universalistic identities are strongly linked to the Greens, the more particularistic identities are correlated with reduced support for the Greens.

5.3 Discussion

Previous sections showed that the "raw material" for a new cleavage in terms of structural foundations and identity potentials looks similar across the countries we study. This section shed light on the role of political agency in the way that a new cleavage becomes organized into the party system. Contrasting a case of early party-strategic realignment – Switzerland – with a case of late realignment – Germany – indicates that the timing and strength with which new voter–party links emerge matters for how fully typical "universalistic" and "particularistic" identity divides are mapped onto the party system. Swiss voters are more likely than German voters to subjectively perceive electoral realignment along the new cleavage lines, in the sense that the Far Right is associated with the working class and the New Left increasingly with a "cosmopolitan" educated middle class. This is especially pronounced among younger voters, who were politically socialized in an already transformed party system.

Looking at specific parties, the comparison of the Swiss and German Social Democrats points to the role of political agency. The Swiss Social Democrats' early and pronounced New Left stance is reflected in how, today, they success-fully challenge or even outperform the Greens as the main perceived representa-tive of universalist groups (cosmopolitans, people with migration background). In Germany, the Social Democrats have ceded this role to the Greens. Relatedly, the mainstream Right in Germany, which partly absorbed a Far Right electoral potential for many years, is more tightly associated with particularist "national" or "down-to-earth" identities than the mainstream right in Switzerland.

Zooming out again from the consideration of specific parties and their histories of mobilization, this section suggests that the structurally rooted identity potentials traced in previous sections find political expression across different contexts, even if the exact form that this takes may vary and obscure common tendencies: Whether it be through the Social Democrats or the Greens, or – at the other end of the political spectrum – a fully-fledged Far Right party or wings of the mainstream Right, the evidence presented in the sections of this Element jointly suggests that a structurally rooted potential for a universalist–particularist identity antagonism in advanced democracies underlies current patterns of party competition in strikingly similar ways, and tends to come to the political fore sooner or later.

6 Conclusion

6.1 Synopsis

European electoral politics appears chaotic these days, marked by high volatility and fragmented party landscapes. The governability of European democracies is seemingly at risk. However, this Element argues against chaos, revealing a structured aspect in contemporary European electoral democracy. That structure takes the form of *constrained volatility*, with voters switching parties within blocks rather than crossing them. The engine is a new cleavage, a particularistic–universalistic divide that is now shaping party systems across Western Europe, as shown for England, France, Germany, and Switzerland in this Element. This cleavage is not necessarily represented by a single party, but instead is expressed in ideological blocks, pitting the universalistic Left against the particularistic Far Right.

Our contribution emphasizes the interplay between cleavage structures and – as the key to understanding party system change in Europe – group identities, situated between social structures and parties, which illuminate how social groups navigate politics amid system fragmentation. In today's complex world, the identity layer is both intricate and irreducible. A key finding here is that in the knowledge economy, structural material interests align with cultural identities. Relative winners and losers in this economy differ materially, but their identities revolve around cultural beliefs, values, and openness much more so than structural positions.

6.2 Scrutinizing the Evidence and Countering Alternative Explanations

Our contentions are clear, but how valid, robust, and believable are they? We answer this question in two different ways. First, we discuss what kinds of evidence would have undermined our hypothesis of a new cleavage. Second, we discuss the relative merits of our account of contemporary European electoral democracies relative to others.

Cleavages imply structured conflict. Our hypothesis about the emergence of the particularistic–universalist cleavage would have fared poorly had markers of structure been absent. Specifically, poor coherence between identity items, weak connections to structural factors, and weak effects on electoral behavior would have been problematic. In our identity-based account, we should expect identities toward different groups to show some structure, and they do. We would also expect socio-structural factors such as education, geography, and occupation to drive group identities. They do. Finally, for any of this to be relevant for party systems, we should find that group identities account for party preferences. Again, they do.

Our hypothesis of a new cleavage would also have taken on water if it does not generalize. This Element builds on our earlier work regarding Switzerland (Bornschier et al. 2021). If we had found that England, France, and Germany function completely differently, then claims of a new European cleavage would have been premature at best. But we find remarkable consistency across the four European countries we study. Given their vast differences on many dimensions (e.g., trajectories of change, past cleavage structures, and institutional political systems), we are reassured that the hypothesis generalizes well in space.

Moving to alternative explanations, we focus on the possible criticism that one does not need both cleavages *and* identities to understand contemporary politics; understanding one suffices. In an age when discussions of identity politics are all the rage, some would undoubtedly argue that it suffices to understand identities. One form such an account could take is to build on the literatures on identity frames (e.g., Bos et al. 2020) and political entrepreneurship (De Vries and Hobolt 2020). Political entrepreneurs with the single-minded goal of winning elections look to mobilize social identities. To that end, they frame grievances and solutions in terms of those identities. The electorate is responsive to those frames, since they put into clear terms what is wrong with society, who is to blame (the out-group), and why the stakes are high (one's very essence as an in-group member is being threatened). By itself, the account does not generate a prediction of constrained volatility. However, building on similar ideas as those concerning issue contagion (e.g., Böhmelt et al. 2016), one could argue that some frames are electorally more successful than others. Arguably, the frame proving to be most successful these days is that pitting particularism against universalism. Consequently, we see some stability despite considerable noise.

We believe that acknowledging the importance of identities by no means makes a more structuralist cleavage theory redundant. While we do not doubt that identity frames play a crucial role or that political entrepreneurs shape the electoral discourse around group identities, our point is that the mobilization markets for different identities are constrained and that the constraints emanate from the fact that identities and the structural potentials that allow these identities to resonate are intertwined. To do away with cleavages, then, would be to forego understanding why certain identity frames succeed and others fail.

Just like some might want to do away with cleavages, other scholars might want to do away with identities. If identities are simply intermediaries between cleavages and electoral decisions, cannot we simply disregard them? We believe, however, that the full story of restructuration requires a consideration of identities. As we have stated, group identities are very much a part of politics, and the reason is that they give meaning to politics and produce stable partisan allegiances. They also allow us to understand how political meanings have changed over time. How can we otherwise understand that the manual working class has not only changed its partisan allegiance but also the group identities it considers as most relevant? It is because their grievances are translated into different identities. In the past, the out-group may have been the wealthy. Increasingly, it would seem to be immigrants. A purely structuralist account would be unable to account for this and would derive erroneous conclusions from a purely materialist analysis of new grievances and inequalities. In addition, from a policy perspective, only if we know how voters think of themselves and others in the political space can we understand their political claims and demands.

A third alternative account focuses on cross-pressures to understand volatility. Here, too, the focus is on socio-structural characteristics rather than identities. The idea is that different socio-structural ascriptions can conflict with each other. These kinds of cross-pressures may cause voters to delay their vote decisions, to respond more intensely to the campaign, and to switch votes more quickly (see Berelson, Lazarsfeld, and McPhee 1954). Depending on the mix of voters, in terms of cross-pressurization, one could observe varying levels of electoral volatility (see also Dassonneville 2022, who considers cross-pressures along the entire "funnel of causality" leading to voting). For this account to be compatible with the empirical patterns we observe, the cross-pressures would have to be very specific, resulting in much more within-block than cross-block volatility. That would seem quite unlikely. We believe group identities – specifically universalistic–particularistic ones that are emerging as particularly salient – to be the reason why cross-pressures, when they occur, do not result in willy-nilly volatility. As we demonstrated, identity formation is rather clearcut in relation to socio-structural characteristics. This explains the pattern of volatility in our country cases.

In sum, we believe that the analysis of both social structure and identities is needed to understand the nature of electoral politics in Europe. The combination explains why we observe constrained volatility instead of complete stability or unstructured chaos. Aside from fitting the data, we also believe our account to be parsimonious. But what does it mean theoretically?

6.3 Toward a New Cleavage Theory

Our account positions us squarely in a structuralist tradition. But it is not a classical structuralist position. We reject the idea that one can either forego social-structural or identity conflict when studying (contemporary European) politics. We need both the political sociology of cleavages and the political psychology of identities.

Both elements found a home in the original formulation of cleavage theory (Lipset and Rokkan 1967). However, in the subsequent development of that theory, the identity aspect has often been neglected. We believe this must change.

In Section 1, we introduced a figure summarizing the shape of the Element and the core of our theoretical argument (Figure 1). We argued that social structures create a potential for groups with clear identities and shared ideological schemas. We argued these notions of group belonging affect party choice but also that political parties influence collective identities and ideological schemas. We now elaborate on these ideas, which we shall dub *the new cleavage theory*. We choose that name not just because of the new cleavage we identified but also because we add new elements to cleavage theory.

We summarize the new cleavage theory in five propositions, which derive from our theoretical apparatus and the findings we have presented. The *first proposition* of the theory is that social structures produce grievances and interests that might affect political behavior. These structures change relatively slowly, resulting in a stable political foundation. However, not all grievances and interests will become politicized.

Second, the politicization of socio-structural conflicts requires the formation of clear group identities. In classical cleavage theory, there is a straightforward mapping of identities onto social structure. A factory worker, for instance, comes to identify with the working class. Moreover, it is especially this in-group identity that matters politically. We deviate from that account in two important ways. First, there often are conceptual degrees of separation between group identities and socio-structural characteristics. The factory worker may identify as a down-to-earth individual more so than as working class, as indeed is often the case in the knowledge economy. Second, out-group identities are every bit as important as in-group identities. The factory worker may feel close to down-to-earth individuals and far removed from cosmopolitans. The worker's party choice may be driven more by their disdain of cosmopolitans than by their love of down-to-earth people.

The third proposition – one we did not really test here – is that political parties use identity frames and ideological schemata to translate grievances into choices. They identify whose interest they cater for (in-group), who is to blame (out-group), and what policy solutions will address the grievances (ideological schemas). Ultimately, of course, they claim sole ownership over those solutions, enticing voters to cast their ballots for them rather than other parties. As a corollary, political parties compete over identity frames. One party might emphasize that the plight of losers in the knowledge economy are the wealthy. Another party may blame it on immigrants. These frames connect to vastly different ideological schemata, in this example, left-wing versus Far Right schemata.

The fourth proposition is that of frame alignment. Not all identity frames and ideological schemata can be expected to mobilize voters. The frames must tell a coherent story that plausibly fits the socio-structural characteristics of a group, which resonates with the "common sense" (Damhuis and Westheuser 2023) of particular socio-structural milieus. Since mass parties cater to numerous clienteles, it is not always possible to tell such a coherent story. However, the idea that political parties can mobilize any identity is implausible.

The final proposition has to do with the peculiarities of the new cleavage between particularism and universalism. That cleavage does not neatly map onto single parties but rather onto ideological blocks. Universalistic identities can be found in several political parties, whose unifying characteristic is that they tend to be New Left. Similarly, particularistic identities can be found across the Far Right. Consequently, it is possible that voters have allegiances to multiple parties within a block, which could translate into volatility. At the same time, the likelihood of cross-block allegiances, especially between parties from the New Left and the Far Right, is quite low because that would require opposing identities within one and the same individual.

6.4 Whence European Politics?

Is Europe destined for political chaos? Increased volatility has many drivers beyond those discussed in this Element, including declining trust in politics and greater protest voting. The idea of constrained volatility implies that things will neither be perfectly stable nor completely chaotic. In this context, it is important to point out that we conducted our surveys in the aftermath of several major events, including the COVID-19 pandemic in all our countries, and Brexit in one of them. If chaos did not ensue in that context, this bodes well for relative stability in the future.

As the particularistic–universalistic cleavage is taking hold of European politics, we can expect polarization to increase. Debates are often heated and compromises more difficult to find when it comes to such cultural values as nationalism versus cosmopolitanism. Affective polarization – the dislike and distrust, and in extreme cases, the villainization of parties and blocks other than one's own – is no longer a curiosity of American politics, but a prominent feature of European politics as well (Gidron, Adams, and Horne 2020; Wagner 2021; Bantel 2023).

Can European democracy withstand this level of polarization? To see where Europe may be headed, it might be useful to revisit the conflicts that dominated twentieth-century European politics, namely, those related to class and nation. These conflicts, too, were highly polarized and involved strong identities. We also witnessed very different trajectories depending on location. The conflict between labor and capital was resolved in many places through compromises among elites, including social-democratic elites. Those gave rise to a softer, tamed form of capitalism, characterized by welfare state policies, and efforts to support employment and earnings capacity (e.g., Hall 2022). The conflict over nationhood, by contrast, gave rise to fascist movements in much of Europe. In some countries, those movements remained at the fringes of politics. In Germany and Italy, they rose to power in weak democratic polities with consequences amply documented. The resolution here came only after much bloodshed and devastating warfare.

How will the particularistic–universalist conflict play out? We are not fortunetellers, but two factors appear to be of crucial importance. The first is institutional capacity – the ability to resolve conflicts and find compromises in governments and legislatures. The second is democratic commitment – the willingness of stakeholders to resolve conflicts democratically or, less demanding, to let those conflicts escalate within the walls of the democratic edifice. On both fronts, there are encouraging and discouraging elements. First, solid institutional foundations remain in place. On the other hand, increased party fragmentation makes it ever more difficult to create governments or find majorities in legislatures. Second, support for democracy remains strong in most European countries. However, it has been eroding in some countries and patience with the democratic process seems to be wearing thinner. More disturbingly, anti-elite and anti-democratic rhetoric have waxed with the populist tide, and intolerance of antagonistic political groups is now a prominent feature in different realms of European politics, threatening liberal democracy.

Ultimately, the trivial truth is that politics is about much more than the identities, opinions, and voting behavior we have discussed in this Element. To fully assess the future of European democracy one would have to consider institutions, elites, international developments/organizations, and many other factors. From a mass perspective, we can say that party systems are in transition. With that comes a degree of volatility, coupled with frictions and animosities. There is limited potential energy here that could turn into a disruptive force. Whether it will depends on the strength of institutions, democratic commitments, and the democratic representation of the group identities that are relevant to voters.

References

Abou-Chadi, Tarik, and Simon Hix (2021). "Brahmin Left versus Merchant Right? Education, Class, Multiparty Competition, and Redistribution in Western Europe." *The British Journal of Sociology* 72(1): 79–92.

Abou-Chadi, Tarik, and Werner Krause (2018). "The Causal Effect of Radical Right Success on Mainstream Parties' Policy Positions: A Regression Discontinuity Approach." *British Journal of Political Science* 50(3): 829–47.

Abrassart, Aurélien, and Stefan C. Wolter (2023). "Rejecting Education as the Basis of the Social Prestige of Occupations: The Role of Polarized Political Ideologies and Parties in Switzerland." *Acta Politica* 58(1): 1–35.

Achen, Christopher H., and Larry M. Bartels (2016). *Democracy for Realists: Why Elections Do Not Produce Responsive Government.* Princeton: Princeton University Press.

Adams, James, Catherine E. de Vries, and Debra Leiter (2011). "Subconstituency Reactions to Elite Depolarization in the Netherlands: An Analysis of the Dutch Public's Policy Beliefs and Partisan Loyalties, 1986–98." *British Journal of Political Science* 42: 81–105.

Ahler, Douglas J., and Gaurav Sood (2018). "The Parties in Our Heads: Misperceptions about Party Composition and Their Consequences." *The Journal of Politics* 80(3): 964–81.

Antonio, Robert (2000). "After Postmodernism: Reactionary Tribalism." *American Journal of Sociology* 106(2): 40–87.

Ares, Macarena, and Mathilde M. van Ditmars (2023). "Intergenerational Social Mobility, Political Socialization and Support for the Left under Post-Industrial Realignment." *British Journal of Political Science* 53 (2): 536–54.

Arzheimer, Kai (2009). "Contextual Factors and the Extreme Right Vote in Western Europe, 1980–2002." *American Journal of Political Science* 53(2): 259–75.

Attewell, David (2021). "Deservingness Perceptions, Welfare State Support and Vote Choice in Western Europe." *West European Politics* 44(3): 611–34.

Autor, David H., and David Dorn (2013). "The Growth of Low-Skill Service Jobs and the Polarization of the US Labor Market." *American Economic Review* 103(5): 1553–97.

Bale, Tim, and Cristóbal Rovira Kaltwasser, eds. (2021). *Riding the Populist Wave: Europe's Mainstream Right in Crisis.* Cambridge: Cambridge University Press.

Bantel, Ivo. (2023). "Camps, Not Just Parties: The Dynamic Foundations of Affective Polarization in Multi-Party Systems." *Electoral Studies* 83(June). www.sciencedirect.com/science/article/pii/S0261379423000367.

Bartolini, Stefano (2000). "The Political Mobilization of the European Left, 1860–1980: The Class Cleavage." Cambridge: Cambridge University Press.

Bartolini, Stefano (2005a). *Restructuring Europe: Centre Formation, System Building and Political Structuring between the Nation-State and the European Union.* Oxford: Oxford University Press.

Bartolini, Stefano (2005b). "La Formations Des Clivages." *Revue Internationale de Politique Comparée* 12(1): 9–34.

Bartolini, Stefano, and Peter Mair (1990). I*dentity, Competition and Electoral Availability: The Stabilisation of European Electorates 1885–1985.* Cambridge: Cambridge University Press.

Beramendi, Pablo, Silja Häusermann, Herbert Kitschelt, and Hanspeter Kriesi (2015). *The Politics of Advanced Capitalism.* New York: Cambridge University Press.

Berelson, Bernard R., Paul F. Lazarsfeld, and Willam N. McPhee (1954). *Voting: A Study of Opinion Formation in a Presidential Campaign.* Chicago: University of Chicago Press.

Betz, Hans-Georg (1994). *Radical Right-Wing Populism in Western Europe.* Basingstoke: Macmillan.

Betz, Hans-Georg (2004). *La Droite Populiste En Europe: Extrême et Démocrate?* Paris: Autrement.

Betz, Hans-Georg, and Carol Johnson (2004). "Against the Current – Stemming the Tide: The Nostalgic Ideology of the Contemporary Radical Populist Right." *Journal of Political Ideologies* 9(3): 311–27.

Böhmelt, Tobias, Lawrence Ezrow, Roni Lehrer, and Hugh Ward (2016). "Party Policy Diffusion." *American Political Science Review* 110 (2): 397–410.

Bolet, Diane (2020). "Local Labour Market Competition and Radical Right Voting: Evidence from France." *European Journal of Political Research* 59(4): 817–41.

Bolet, Diane (2021). "Drinking Alone: Local Socio-Cultural Degradation and Radical Right Support – The Case of British Pub Closures." *Comparative Political Studies* 54(9): 1653–92.

Bornschier, Simon (2009). "Cleavage Politics in Old and New Democracies." *Living Reviews in Democracy* 1(1): 1–13.

Bornschier, Simon (2010). *Cleavage Politics and the Populist Right: The New Cultural Conflict in Western Europe.* Philadelphia: Temple University Press.

Bornschier, Simon (2012). "Why a Right-Wing Populist Party Emerged in France but Not in Germany: Cleavages and Actors in the Formation of a New Cultural Divide." *European Political Science Review* 4(1): 121–45.

Bornschier, Simon (2017). "Populist Mobilization across Time and Space: An Introduction." *Swiss Political Science Review* 23(4): 301–12.

Bornschier, Simon (2018). "Globalization, Cleavages, and the Radical Right." In *The Oxford Handbook of the Radical Right*, edited by Jens Rydgren. New York: Oxford University Press, 212–38.

Bornschier, Simon, and Hanspeter Kriesi (2013). "The Populist Right, the Working Class, and the Changing Face of Class Politics." In *Class Politics and the Radical Right*, edited by Jens Rydgren. Abingdon: Routledge, 10–29.

Bornschier, Simon, Silja Häusermann, Delia Zollinger, and Céline Colombo (2021). "How 'Us' and 'Them' Relates to Voting Behavior – Social Structure, Social Identities, and Electoral Choice." *Comparative Political Studies* 54(12): 2087–122.

Bos, Linda, Christian Schemer, Nicoleta Corbu et al. (2020). "The Effects of Populism as a Social Identity Frame on Persuasion and Mobilisation: Evidence from a 15-Country Experiment." *European Journal of Political Research* 59(1): 3–24.

Bourdieu, Pierre (1984). *Distinction: A Social Critique of the Judgment of Taste*. Cambridge, MA: Harvard University Press.

Bourdieu, Pierre (1985). "The Social Space and the Genesis of Groups." *Theory and Society* 14(6): 723–44.

Bremer, Björn, and Julia Schulte-Cloos (2019). "The Restructuring of British and German Party Politics in Times of Crisis." In *European Party Politics in Times of Crisis*, edited by Swen Hutter and Hanspeter Kriesi. Cambridge: Cambridge University Press, 281–301.

Breyer, Magdalena, Tabea Palmtag, and Delia Zollinger (2023). "Narratives of Backlash? Perceptions of Changing Status Hierarchies in Open-Ended Survey Responses." *URPP Equality of Opportunity Discussion Paper Series* No.15.

Burgoon, Brian, Sam van Noort, Matthijs Rooduijn, and Geoffrey Underhill (2019). "Positional Deprivation and Support for Radical Right and Radical Left Parties." *Economic Policy* 34(97): 49–93.

Busch, Kathrin (2016). "Estimating Parties' Left-Right Positions: Determinants of Voters' Perceptions' Proximity to Party Ideology." *Electoral Studies* 41: 159–78.

Cameron, James E. (2004). "A Three-Factor Model of Social Identity." *Self and Identity* 3(3): 239–62.

Carella, Leonardo, and Robert Ford (2020). "The Status Stratification of Radical Right Support: Reconsidering the Occupational Profile of UKIP's Electorate." *Electoral Studies* 67: 102214. www.sciencedirect.com/science/article/pii/S0261379420300950.

Carter, Elisabeth (2005). *The Extreme Right in Western Europe: Success or Failure?* Manchester: Manchester University Press.

Chhibber, Pradeep, and Mariano Torcal (1997). "Elite Strategy, Social Cleavages, and Party Systems in a New Democracy: Spain." *Comparative Political Studies* 30(1): 27–54.

Conover, Pamela J. (1988). "The Role of Social Groups in Political Thinking." *British Journal of Political Science* 18(1): 51–76.

Coser, Lewis A. (1956). *The Functions of Social Conflict. An Examination of the Concept of Social Conflict and Its Use in Empirical Sociological Research*. New York: The Free Press.

Cramer, Katherine J. (2016). *The Politics of Resentment – Rural Consciousness in Wisconsin and the Rise of Scott Walker*. Chicago: University of Chicago Press.

Dalton, Russel J. (2018). *Political Realignment: Economics, Culture and Electoral Change*. Oxford: Oxford University Press.

Dalton, Russell J., and Martin P. Wattenberg, eds. (2002). *Parties without Partisans: Political Change in Advanced Industrial Democracies*. Oxford: Oxford University Press.

Dalton, Russell J., Scott C. Flanagan, and Paul Allen Beck, eds. (1984). *Electoral Change in Advanced Industrial Democracies: Realignment or Dealignment?* Princeton: Princeton University Press.

Damhuis, Koen (2020). *Roads to the Radical Right: Understanding Different Forms of Electoral Support for Radical Right-Wing Parties in France and the Netherlands*. Oxford: Oxford University Press.

Damhuis, Koen, and Linus Westheuser (2023). "Cleavage Politics beyond Ideology: How Common Sense Divides," Manuscript.

Dancygier, Rafaela M., and Stefanie Walter (2015). "Globalization, Labor Market Risks, and Class Cleavages." In *The Politics of Advanced Capitalism*, edited by. Pablo Beramendi, Silja Häusermann, and Herbert Kitschelt. Cambridge: Cambridge University Press, 133–56.

Dassonneville, Ruth (2022). *Voters under Pressure: Group-Based Cross-Pressure and Electoral Volatility*. Oxford: Oxford University Press.

Dassonneville, Ruth, and Marc Hooghe (2017). "Economic Indicators and Electoral Volatility: Economic Effects on Electoral Volatility in Western Europe, 1950–2013." *Comparative European Politics* 15(6): 919–43.

Dassonneville, Ruth, Rune Stubager, and Mads Thau (2022). "The effectiveness of group appeals." Working Paper.

Deegan-Krause, Kevin, and Zsolt Enyedi (2010). "Agency and Structure of Party Competition: Alignment, Stability and the Role of Political Elites." *West European Politics* 33(3): 686–710.

De Jonge, Léonie (2021). *The Success and Failure of Right-Wing Populist Parties in the Benelux Countries*. Abingdon: Routledge.

De Vries, Catherine E., and Sara B. Hobolt (2020). *Political Entrepreneurs: The Rise of Challenger Parties in Europe*. Princeton: Princeton University Press.

De Wilde, Pieter, Ruud Koopmans, Wolfgang Merkel, Oliver Strijbis, and Michael Zürn, eds. (2019). *The Struggle over Borders: Cosmopolitanism and Communitarianism*. Cambridge: Cambridge University Press.

Dolinsky, Alona O. (2023). "Parties' Group Appeals across Time, Countries, and Communication Channels – Examining Appeals to Social Groups via the Parties' Group Appeals Dataset." *Party Politics* 29(6): 1130–46.

Duyvendak, Jan Willem (2011). *The Politics of Home*. London: Palgrave Macmillan.

Elchardus, Mark, and Bram Spruyt (2012). "The Contemporary Contradictions of Egalitarianism: An Empirical Analysis of the Relationship between the Old and New Left/Right Alignments." *European Political Science Review* 4(2): 217–39.

Elgenius, Gabriella, and Jens Rydgren (2019). "Frames of Nostalgia and Belonging: The Resurgence of Ethno-Nationalism in Sweden." *European Societies* 21(4): 583–602.

Elgenius, Gabriella, and Jens Rydgren (2022). "Nationalism and the Politics of Nostalgia." *Sociological Forum* 37(S1): 1230–43.

Emanuele, Vincenzo, and Alessandro Chiaramonte (2018). "A Growing Impact of New Parties: Myth or Reality? Party System Innovation in Western Europe after 1945." *Party Politics* 24(5): 475–87.

Enggist, Matthias, and Michael Pinggera (2021). "Radical Right Parties and Their Welfare State Stances – Not So Blurry after All?" *West European Politics* 45(1): 102–28.

Engler, Sarah, and David Weisstanner (2021) "The Threat of Social Decline: Income Inequality and Radical Right Support." *Journal of European Public Policy* 28(2): 153–73.

Enyedi, Zsolt (2005). "The Role of Agency in Cleavage Formation." *European Journal of Political Research* 44(5): 697–720.

Esping-Andersen, Gøsta (1999). "Politics without Class? Postindustrial Cleavages in Europe and America." In *Continuity and Change in Contemporary Capitalism*, edited by Herbert Kitschelt, Peter Lange, Gary Marks, and John D. Stephens. Cambridge: Cambridge University Press, 293–316.

Evans, Geoffrey, ed. (1999). *The End of Class Politics? Class Voting in Comparative Context*. Oxford: Oxford University Press.

Evans, Geoffrey, and James Tilley. (2011). "How Parties Shape Class Politics: Explaining the Decline of the Class Basis of Party Support." *British Journal of Political Science* 42: 137–61.

Evans, Geoffrey, and Nan Dirk de Graaf, eds. (2013). *Political Choice Matters: Explaining the Strength of Class and Religious Cleavages in Cross-National Perspective.* Oxford: Oxford University Press.

Finney, Patrick (2010). *Remembering the Road to World War Two: International History, National Identity, Collective Memory.* New York: Routledge.

Fitzgerald, Jennifer (2018). *Close to Home: Local Ties and Voting Radical Right in Europe.* Cambridge: Cambridge University Press.

Flemmen, Magne Paalgard, Vegard Jarness, and Lennart Rosenlund (2019). "Class, Lifestyles and Politics: Homologies of Social Position, Taste and Political Stances." In *Empirical Investigations of Social Space*, edited by Jörg Blasius, Frédéric Lebaron, Brigitte Le Roux, and Andreas Schmitz. Cham: Springer, 155–74.

Florida, Richard (2012). *The Rise of the Creative Class, Revisited.* New York: Basic Books.

Franklin, Mark (1992). "The Decline of Cleavage Politics." In *Electoral Change: Responses to Evolving Social Und Attitudinal Structures in Western Countries*, edited by Mark Franklin, Thomas Mackie, and Henry Valen. Cambridge: Cambridge University Press, 383–405.

Franklin, Mark, Thomas Mackie, and Henry Valen, eds. (1992). *Electoral Change: Responses to Evolving Social and Attitudinal Structures in Western Countries.* Cambridge: Cambridge University Press.

Gamson, William A. (1992). "The Social Psychology of Collective Action." In *Frontiers in Social Movement Theory*, edited by Aldon D. Morris and Carol McClurg Mueller. New Haven: Yale University Press, 53–76.

Garritzmann, Julian L., Silja Häusermann, and Bruno Palier (2022a). *The World Politics of Social Investment: Volume I: Welfare States in the Knowledge Economy.* Oxford: Oxford University Press.

Garritzmann, Julian L., Silja Häusermann, Thomas Kurer, Bruno Palier, and Michael Pinggera (2022b). "The Emergence of Knowledge Economies: Educational Expansion, Labor Market Changes, and the Politics of Social Investment." In *The World Politics of Social Investment*, edited by Julian L. Garritzmann, Silja Häusermann, and Bruno Palier. Oxford: Oxford University Press, 251–83.

Garzia, Diego, Frederico Ferreira da Silva, and Andrea De Angelis (2022). "Partisan Dealignment and the Personalisation of Politics in West European Parliamentary Democracies, 1961–2018." *West European Politics* 45(2): 311–34.

Gest, Justin (2016). *The New Minority: White Working Class Politics in an Age of Immigration and Inequality.* New York: Oxford University Press.

Gethin, Amory, Clara Martínez-Toledano, and Thomas Piketty (2021). *Political Cleavages and Social Inequalities: A Study of Fifty Democracies, 1948–2020*. Cambridge, MA: Harvard University Press.

Gidron, Noam, and Daniel Ziblatt (2019). "Center-Right Political Parties in Advanced Democracies." *Annual Review of Political Science* 22(1): 17–35.

Gidron, Noam, and Peter A. Hall (2017). "The Politics of Social Status: Economic and Cultural Roots of the Populist Right." *The British Journal of Sociology* 68: 57–84.

Gidron, Noam, James Adams, and Will Horne (2020). *American Affective Polarization in Comparative Perspective*. Cambridge: Cambridge University Press.

Gingrich, Jane (2019). "Did State Responses to Automation Matter for Voters?" *Research & Politics* 6(1). https://journals.sagepub.com/doi/full/10.1177/2053168019832745.

Gingrich, Jane, and Julia Lynch (2019). "Integrative Institutions and Mainstream Party Collapse: The Regional Context." Paper presented at the Council For European Studies Annual Meeting.

Gingrich, Jane, and Silja Häusermann (2015). "The Decline of the Working-Class Vote, the Reconfiguration of the Welfare Support Coalition and Consequences for the Welfare State." *Journal of European Social Policy* 25(1): 50–75.

Goggin, Stephen N., John A. Henderson, and Alexander G. Theodoridis (2020). "What Goes with Red and Blue? Mapping Partisan and Ideological Associations in the Minds of Voters." *Political Behavior* 42(4): 985–1013.

Golder, Matt (2016). "Far Right Parties in Europe." *Annual Review of Political Science* 19(1): 477–97.

Gougou, Florent, and Simon Persico (2017). "A New Party System in the Making? The 2017 French Presidential Election." *French Politics* 15(3): 303–21.

Green-Pedersen, Christoffer (2007). "The Growing Importance of Issue Competition: The Changing Nature of Party Competition in Western Europe." *Political Studies* 55(3): 607–28.

Green-Pedersen, Christoffer (2019). *Reshaping of West European Party Politics: Agenda-Setting and Party Competition in Comparative Perspective*. Oxford: Oxford University Press.

Hall, Peter A. (2020). "The Electoral Politics of Growth Regimes." *Perspectives on Politics* 18(1): 185–99.

Hall, Peter A. (2021). "How Growth Strategies Evolve in the Developed Democracies." In *Growth and Welfare in the Global Economy: How Growth Regimes Evolve*, edited by Anke Hassel and Bruno Palier. Oxford: Oxford University Press, 57–97.

Hall, Peter A. (2022). "The Shifting Relationship between Post-War Capitalism and Democracy." *Government and Opposition* 57(1): 1–30.

Harteveld, Eelco, Wouter Van Der Brug, Sarah De Lange, and Tom Van Der Meer (2022). "Multiple Roots of the Populist Radical Right: Support for the Dutch PVV in Cities and the Countryside." *European Journal of Political Research* 61(2): 440–61.

Häusermann, Silja, and Hanspeter Kriesi (2015). "What Do Voters Want? Dimensions and Configurations in Individual-Level Preferences and Party Choice." In *The Politics of Advanced Capitalism*, edited by Pablo Beramendi, Silja Häusermann, Herbert Kitschelt, and Hanspeter Kriesi, 202–30. New York: Cambridge University Press.

Häusermann, Silja, and Herbert Kitschelt, eds. (2024). *Beyond Social Democracy: The Transformation of the Left in Emerging Knowledge Societies*. Cambridge: Cambridge University Press.

Häusermann, Silja, Achim Kemmerling, and David Rueda (2020). "How Labor Market Inequality Transforms Mass Politics." *Political Science Research and Methods* 8(2): 344–55.

Häusermann, Silja, Michael Pinggera, Macarena Ares, and Matthias Enggist (2022). "Class and Social Policy in the Knowledge Economy." *European Journal of Political Research* 61(2): 462–84.

Häusermann, Silja, Tarik Abou-Chadi, Reto Bürgisser et al. (2022). *Wählerschaft und Perspektiven der Sozialdemokratie in der Schweiz*. Zürich: NZZ Libro.

Häusermann, Silja, Thomas Kurer, and Hanna Schwander (2014). "High-Skilled Outsiders? Labor Market Vulnerability, Education and Welfare State Preferences." *Socio-Economic Review* 13(2): 235–58.

Häusermann, Silja, Thomas Kurer, and Delia Zollinger (2023). "Aspiration versus Apprehension: Economic Opportunities and Electoral Preferences." *British Journal of Political Science* 53(4): 1230–51.

Hawkins, Kirk A., Ryan E. Carlin, Levente Littvay, and Cristóbal Rovira Kaltwasser, eds. (2018). *The Ideational Approach to Populism: Concept, Theory, and Analysis*. Abingdon: Routledge.

Hegewald, Sven, and Dominik Schraff. (2022). "Place-Based Affect and the Cosmopolitan-Nationalist Divide." Unpublished manuscript, available as preprint at https://osf.io/ab3dg/.

Helbling, Marc, and Sebastian Jungkunz (2020). "Social Divides in the Age of Globalization." *West European Politics* 43(6): 1187–210.

Hobolt, Sara B., Thomas J. Leeper, and James Tilley (2021). "Divided by the Vote: Affective Polarization in the Wake of the Brexit Referendum." *British Journal of Political Science* 51(4): 1476–93.

Hochschild, Arlie R. (2016). *Strangers in Their Own Land*. New York: The New Press.

Hooghe, Liesbet, and Gary Marks (2018). "Cleavage Theory Meets Europe's Crises: Lipset, Rokkan, and the Transnational Cleavage." *Journal of European Public Policy* 25(1): 109–35.

Hooghe, Liesbet, Gary Marks, and Jonne Kamphorst (2022). "Fields of Education and the Transnational Cleavage," manuscript.

Huber, Lena Maria (2022). "Beyond Policy: The Use of Social Group Appeals in Party Communication." *Political Communication* 39(3): 293–310.

Huddy, Leonie (2001). "From Social to Political Identity: A Critical Examination of Social Identity Theory." *Political Psychology* 22(1): 127–56.

Hutter, Swen, and Hanspeter Kriesi, eds. (2019). *European Party Politics in Times of Crisis*. Cambridge: Cambridge University Press.

Ignazi, Piero (1992). "The Silent Counter-Revolution: Hypotheses on the Emergence of Extreme Right-Wing Parties in Europe." *European Journal of Political Research* 22(1): 3–33.

Ignazi, Piero (2020). "The Four Knights of Intra-Party Democracy: A Rescue for Party Delegitimation." *Party Politics* 26: 9–20.

Inglehart, Ronald (1984). "The Changing Structure of Political Cleavages in Western Society." In *Electoral Change in Advanced Industrial Democracies: Realignment or Dealignment?* edited by Russell J. Dalton, Scott C. Flanagan, and Paul Allen Beck. Princeton: Princeton University Press, 25–69.

Iversen, Torben, and David Soskice (2019). *Democracy and Prosperity: Reinventing Capitalism through a Turbulent Century*. Princeton: Princeton University Press.

Iyengar, Shanto, Gaurav Sood, and Yphtach Lelkes (2012). "Affect, Not Ideology: A Social Identity Perspective on Polarization." *Public Opinion Quarterly* 76: 405–31.

Iyengar, Shanto, Yphtach Lelkes, Matthew Levendusky, Neil Malhotra, and Sean J. Westwood (2019). "The Origins and Consequences of Affective Polarization in the United States." *Annual Review of Political Science* 22(1): 129–46.

Jacobs, Nicholas F., and B. Kal Munis (2019). "Place-Based Imagery and Voter Evaluations: Experimental Evidence on the Politics of Place." *Political Research Quarterly* 72(2): 263–77.

Kane, John V., Lilliana Mason, and Julie Wronski (2021). "Who's at the Party? Group Sentiments, Knowledge, and Partisan Identity." *The Journal of Politics* 83(4): 1783–99.

Katz, Richard S., and Peter Mair, eds. (1994). *How Parties Organize: Change and Adaptation in Party Organizations in Western Democracies*. London: Sage.

Katz, Richard S., and Peter Mair (2018). *Democracy and the Cartelization of Political Parties*. Oxford: Oxford University Press.

Kitschelt, Herbert (1988). "Left-Libertarian Parties: Explaining Innovation in Competitive Party Systems." *World Politics* 40(2): 194–234.

Kitschelt, Herbert (1994). *The Transformation of European Social Democracy*. New York: Cambridge University Press.

Kitschelt, Herbert, and Anthony J. McGann (1995). *The Radical Right in Western Europe: A Comparative Analysis*. Ann Arbor: University of Michigan Press.

Kitschelt, Herbert, and Philipp Rehm (2014). "Occupations as a Site of Political Preference Formation." *Comparative Political Studies* 47(12): 1670–706.

Kitschelt, Herbert, and Philipp Rehm (2023). "Polarity Reversal: The Socioeconomic Reconfiguration of Partisan Support in Knowledge Societies." *Politics & Society* 51(4): 520–66. Online ahead of print. https://doi.org/10.1177/00323292221100220.

Klandermans, Bert (2001). "Why Social Movements Come into Being and Why People Join Them." In *The Blackwell Companion to Sociology*, edited by Judith R. Blau. Malden. Mass: Blackwell, 268–81.

Knutsen, Oddbjørn (2004). *Social Structure and Party Choice in Western Europe: A Comparative Longitudinal Study*. Basingstoke: Palgrave-Macmillan.

Knutsen, Oddbjørn, and Elinor Scarbrough (1995). "Cleavage Politics." In *The Impact of Values*, edited by Jan W. van Deth and Elinor Scarbrough. Oxford: Oxford University Press, 492–523.

Kriesi, Hanspeter (1989). "New Social Movements and the New Class in the Netherlands." *American Journal of Sociology* 94(5): 165–85.

Kriesi, Hanspeter (1998). "The Transformation of Cleavage Politics: The 1997 Stein Rokkan Lecture." *European Journal of Political Research* 33(2), 165–85.

Kriesi, Hanspeter (1999). "Movements of the Left, Movements of the Right: Putting the Mobilization of Two New Types of Social Movements into Political Context." In *Continuity and Change in Contemporary Capitalism*, edited by Herbert Kitschelt, Peter Lange, Gary Marks, and John D. Stephens . Cambridge: Cambridge University Press, 398–423.

Kriesi, Hanspeter (2014). "The Populist Challenge." *West European Politics* 37(2): 361–78. https://doi.org/10.1080/01402382.2014.887879.

Kriesi, Hanspeter, Edgar Grande, Martin Dolezal et al. (2012). *Political Conflict in Western Europe*. Cambridge: Cambridge University Press.

Kriesi, Hanspeter, Edgar Grande, Romain Lachat et al. (2008). "West European Politics in the Age of Globalization." Cambridge: Cambridge University Press.

Kurer, Thomas (2020). "The Declining Middle: Occupational Change, Social Status, and the Populist Right." *Comparative Political Studies* 53(10–11): 1798–835.

Kurer, Thomas, and Briitta Van Staalduinen (2022). "Disappointed Expectations: Downward Mobility and Electoral Change." *American Political Science Review* 116(4): 1340–56. https://doi.org/10.1017/S0003055422000077.

Kurer, Thomas, and Bruno Palier (2019). "Shrinking and Shouting: The Political Revolt of the Declining Middle in Times of Employment Polarization." *Research & Politics* 6(1): 1–6. https://doi.org/10.1177/2053168019831164.

Lamont, Michèle (2000). *The Dignity of Working Men: Morality and the Boundaries of Race, Class, and Immigration*. New York: Russel Sage Foundation.

Lamont, Michèle, and Virág Molnár (2002). "The Study of Boundaries in the Social Sciences." *Annual Review of Sociology* 28(1): 167–95.

Lijphart, Arend (1979). "Religious vs. Linguistic vs. Class Voting: The 'Crucial Experiment' of Comparing Belgium, Canada, South Africa and Switzerland." *American Political Science Review* 73(2): 442–58.

Lipset, Seymour Martin, and Stein Rokkan (1967). "Cleavage Structures, Party Systems, and Voter Alignments: An Introduction." In *Party Systems and Voter Alignments*, edited by Seymour Martin Lipset and Stein Rokkan. New York: The Free Press, 1–64.

Lorenzini, Jasmine, and Mathilde M. van Ditmars (2019). "Austria, France, the Netherlands and Switzerland: Old and New Winning Formulas of the Populist Radical Right." In *European Party Politics in Times of Crisis*, edited by Swen Hutter and Hanspeter Kriesi. Cambridge: Cambridge University Press, 261–80.

Mair, Peter (1997). *Party System Change: Approaches and Interpretations*. Oxford: Clarendon Press.

Mair, Peter (2013). *Ruling the Void: The Hollowing of Western Democracy*. London: Verso Books.

Manow, Philip. (2018). *Die Politische Ökonomie Des Populismus*. Berlin: Suhrkamp.

Marino, Bruno, Nicola Martocchia Diodati, and Luca Verzichelli (2022). "The Personalization of Party Politics in Western Europe (1985–2016): Evidence from an Expert Survey." *Acta Politica* 57(3): 571–96.

Marks, Gary (1989). *Unions in Politics: Britain, Germany, and the United States in the Nineteenth and Early Twentieth Centuries*. Princeton: Princeton University Press.

Marks, Gary, Liesbet Hooghe, Moira Nelson, and Erica Edwards (2006). "Party Competition and European Integration in the East and West: Different Structure, Same Causality." *Comparative Political Studies* 39: 155–75.

Marks, Gary, Attewell David, Liesbet Hooghe, Jan Rovny, and Marco Steenbergen (2023). "The Social Bases of Political Parties: A New Measure and Survey." *British Journal of Political Science* 53: 249–60.

Marx, Karl (1937 [1852]). *The Eighteenth Brumaire of Louis Bonaparte.* Moscow: Progress.

Mason, Lilliana (2018). *Uncivil Agreement – How Politics Became Our Identity.* Chicago: University of Chicago Press.

Mason, Lilliana, and Julie Wronski (2018). "One Tribe to Bind Them All: How Our Social Group Attachments Strengthen Partisanship." *Political Psychology* 39: 257–77. https://doi.org/10.1111/pops.12485.

Maxwell, Rahsaan (2019). "Cosmopolitan Immigration Attitudes in Large European Cities: Contextual or Compositional Effects?" *American Political Science Review* 672: 1–19. https://doi.org/10.1017/S0003055418000898.

Meguid, Bonnie M. (2008). *Party Competition between Unequals: Strategies and Electoral Fortunes in Western Europe.* Cambridge: Cambridge University Press.

Meyer, Thomas M, and Markus Wagner (2020). "Perceptions of Parties' Left-Right Positions: The Impact of Salience Strategies." *Party Politics* 26(5): 664–74.

Mierke-Zatwarnicki, Alex (2022). "Varieties of identity politics: A macro-historical approach." Working Paper.

Minkenberg, Michael (2000). "The Renewal of the Radical Right: Between Modernity and Anti-Modernity." *Government and Opposition* 35(2): 170–88.

Minkenberg, Michael, and Pascal Perrineau (2007). "The Radical Right in the European Elections 2004." *International Political Science Review* 28(1): 29–55.

Mudde, Cas (2000). *The Ideology of the Extreme Right.* Manchester: Manchester University Press.

Nasr, Mohamed (2020). "Voter Perceptions of Parties' Left–Right Positions: The Role of Party Strategies." *Electoral Studies* 68: 102239. https://doi.org/10.1016/j.electstud.2020.102239.

Norris, Pippa, and Ronald Inglehart (2019). *Cultural Backlash: Trump, Brexit and Authoritarian Populism.* Cambridge: Cambridge University Press.

Oesch, Daniel (2006a). *Redrawing the Class Map: Stratification and Institutions in Britain, Germany, Sweden and Switzerland.* Basingstoke: Palgrave Macmillan.

Oesch, Daniel (2006b). "Coming to Grips with a Changing Class Structure: An Analysis of Employment Stratification in Britain, Germany, Sweden and

Switzerland." *International Sociology* 21(2): 263–88. https://doi.org/ 10.1177/0268580906061379.

Oesch, Daniel (2013). *Occupational Change in Europe: How Technology and Education Transform the Job Structure*. Oxford: Oxford University Press.

Oesch, Daniel, and Line Rennwald (2018). "Electoral Competition in Europe's New Tripolar Political Space: Class Voting for the Left, Centre-Right and Radical Right." *European Journal of Political Research* (January) 57(4): 783–807. https://doi.org/10.1111/1475-6765.12259.

Off, Gefjon (2023). "Gender Equality Salience, Backlash and Radical Right Voting in the Gender-Equal Context of Sweden." *West European Politics* 46(3): 451–76.

Oskarson, Maria, Henrik Oscarsson, and Edvin Boije (2016). "Consideration and Choice: Analyzing Party Choice in the Swedish European Election 2014." *Scandinavian Political Studies* 39(3): 242–63.

Patana, Pauliina (2022). "Residential Constraints and the Political Geography of the Populist Radical Right: Evidence from France." *Perspectives on Politics* 20(3): 842–59.

Pirro, Andrea L. P. (2023). "Far Right: The Significance of an Umbrella Concept." *Nations and Nationalism* 29(1): 101–12.

Pless, Anna, Paul Tromp, and Dick Houtman (2023). "Religious and Secular Value Divides in Western Europe: A Cross-National Comparison (1981–2008)." *International Political Science Review* 44(2): 178–94.

Poguntke, Thomas (1987). "New Politics and Party Systems: The Emergence of a New Type of Party?" *West European Politics* 10(1): 76–88.

Poguntke, Thomas (2002). "Party Organizational Linkage: Parties without Firm Social Roots?" In *Political Parties in the New Europe*, edited by Kurt Richard Luther and Ferdinand Müller-Rommel. Oxford: Oxford University Press, 43–62.

Poguntke, Thomas, and Paul Webb, eds. (2005). *The Presidentialization of Politics: A Comparative Study of Modern Democracies*. Oxford: Oxford University Press.

Powell, Walter W., and Kaisa Snellman (2004). "The Knowledge Economy." *Annual Review of Sociology* 30: 199–220.

Rathgeb, Philip, and Marius R. Busemeyer (2022). "The Radical Right and Welfare Politics: Causes and Consequences." *West European Politics* 45(1): 1–23. https://doi.org/10.1080/01402382.2021.1925421.

Reiljan, Andres (2020). "'Fear and Loathing across Party Lines' (Also) in Europe: Affective Polarisation in European Party Systems." *European Journal of Political Research* 59(2): 376–96. https://doi.org/10.1111/1475-6765 .12351.

Rennwald, Line, and Geoffrey Evans (2014). "When Supply Creates Demand: Social Democratic Party Strategies and the Evolution of Class Voting." *West European Politics* 37(5): 1108–35.

Ridgeway, Cecilia L. (2019). *Status: Why Is It Everywhere? Why Does It Matter?* New York: Russel Sage Foundation.

Robison, Joshua, Rune Stubager, Mads Thau, and James Tilley (2021). "Does Class-Based Campaigning Work? How Working Class Appeals Attract and Polarize Voters." *Comparative Political Studies* 54(5): 723–52.

Roccas, Sonia, and Marilynn B. Brewer (2002). "Social Identity Complexity." *Personality and Social Psychology Review* 6(2): 88–106.

Rokkan, Stein (1999). *State Formation, Nation-Building, and Mass Politics in Europe: The Theory of Stein Rokkan, Based on His Collected Works*, edited by Peter Flora with Stein Kuhnle and Derek Urwin. Oxford: Oxford University Press.

Rooduijn, Matthijs, and Brian Burgoon (2018). "The Paradox of Well-Being: Do Unfavorable Socioeconomic and Sociocultural Contexts Deepen or Dampen Radical Left and Right Voting among the Less Well-Off?" *Comparative Political Studies* 51(13): 1720–53.

Rose, Richard, and I. McAllister (1986). *Voters Begin to Choose: From Closed-Class to Open Elections in Britain*. London: Sage.

Rueda, David (2005). "Insider–Outsider Politics in Industrialized Democracies: The Challenge to Social Democratic Parties." *American Political Science Review* 99(1): 61–74.

Rydgren, Jens (2005). "Is Extreme Right-Wing Populism Contagious? Explaining the Emergence of a New Party Family." *European Journal of Political Research* 44(3): 413–37.

Rydgren, Jens (2007). "The Sociology of the Radical Right." *Annual Review of Sociology* 33(1): 241–62.

Rydgren, Jens (2013). *Class Politics and the Radical Right*. Abingdon: Routledge.

Sartori, Giovanni (1968). "The Sociology of Parties: A Critical Review." In *Party Systems, Party Organizations, and the Politics of New Masses*, edited by Otto Stammer. Berlin: Freie Universität Berlin, 1–25.

Savage, Mike (2015). *Class in the 21st Century*. London: Pelican Books.

Savage, Mike, Fiona Devine, Niall Cunningham et al. (2013). "A New Model of Social Class? Findings from the BBC's Great British Class Survey Experiment." *Sociology* 47(2): 219–50.

Sczepanski, Ronja (2022). "Who are the cosmopolitans? How perceived social sorting and social identities relate to European and national identities." Working Paper.

Shayo, Moses (2009). "A Model of Social Identity with an Application to Political Economy: Nation, Class, and Redistribution." *American Political Science Review* 103(2): 147–74.

Snow, David A., and Doug McAdam (2000). "Identity Work Processes in the Context of Social Movements: Clarifying the Identity/Movement Nexus." In *Self, Identity, and Social Movements*, edited by Sheldon Stryker, Timothy J. Owens, and Robert W. White. Minneapolis: University of Minnesota Press, 41–67.

Snow, David A., E. Burke Rochford, Steven K. Worden, and Robert D. Benford (1986). "Frame Alignment Processes, Micromobilization, and Movement Participation." *American Sociological Review* 51(4): 464–81.

Spoon, Jae-Jae, and Heike Klüver (2019). "Party Convergence and Vote Switching: Explaining Mainstream Party Decline across Europe." *European Journal of Political Research* 58(4): 1021–42.

Spoon, Jae-Jae, and Heike Klüver (2020). "Responding to Far Right Challengers: Does Accommodation Pay Off?" *Journal of European Public Policy* 27(2): 273–91.

Steenbergen, Marco R., and Thomas Willi (2019). "What Consideration Sets Can Teach Us about Electoral Competition: A Two-Hurdle Model." *Electoral Studies* 57: 263–74.

Steenbergen, Marco R., Dominik Hangartner, and Catherine E. De Vries (2015). "The Adaptive Voter: Choice Sets and Party Competition in the 1988 and 1992 U.S. Presidential Elections."

Steiner, Nils D., Matthias Mader, and Harald Schoen (2024). "Subjective Losers of Globalization." *European Journal of Political Research* 63(1): 326–47. Online ahead of print. https://onlinelibrary.wiley.com/doi/abs/10.1111/1475-6765 .12603.

Stryker, Sheldon (1980). *Symbolic Interactionism: A Social Structural Version*. Menlo Park: Benjamin Cummings.

Stryker, Sheldon (2000). "Identity Competition: Key to Differential Social Movement Participation?" In *Self, Identity, and Social Movements*, edited by Sheldon Stryker, Timothy J Owens, and Robert W White. Minneapolis: University of Minnesota Press, 21–39.

Stubager, Rune (2008). "Education Effects on Authoritarian-Libertarian Values: A Question of Socialization." *British Journal of Sociology* 59(2): 327–50.

Stubager, Rune (2009). "Education-Based Group Identity and Consciousness in the Authoritarian-Libertarian Value Conflict." *European Journal of Political Research* 48(2): 204–33.

Stuckelberger, Simon, and Anke Tresch (2022). "Group Appeals of Parties in Times of Economic and Identity Conflicts and Realignment." *Political Studies*. Online ahead of print. https://doi.org/10.1177/00323217221123147.

Tajfel, Henri (1981). *Human Groups and Social Categories*. New York: Cambridge University Press.

Tajfel, Henri, and John C. Turner (1979). "An Integrative Theory of Intergroup Conflict." In *The Social Psychology of Intergroup Relations*, edited by William G. Austin and Stephen Worchel. Monterey: Brooks/Cole, 33–48.

Thau, Mads (2019). "How Political Parties Use Group-Based Appeals: Evidence from Britain 1964–2015." *Political Studies* 67(1): 63–82.

Thau, Mads (2021). "The Social Divisions of Politics: How Parties' Group-Based Appeals Influence Social Group Differences in Vote Choice." *The Journal of Politics* 83(2): 675–88.

Thijssen, Peter, and Pieter Verheyen (2022). "It's All about Solidarity Stupid! How Solidarity Frames Structure the Party Political Sphere." *British Journal of Political Science* 52(1): 128–45.

Titelman, Noam, and Benjamin E. Lauderdale (2023). "Can Citizens Guess How Other Citizens Voted Based on Demographic Characteristics?" *Political Science Research and Methods* 11(2): 254–74.

Van de Werfhorst, Herman G., and Gerbert Kraaykamp (2001). "Four Field-Related Educational Resources and Their Impact on Labor, Consumption, and Sociopolitical Orientation." *Sociology of Education*, 74(4): 296–317.

van Spanje, Joost (2010). "Contagious Parties: Anti-Immigration Parties and Their Impact on Other Parties' Immigration Stances in Contemporary Western Europe." *Party Politics* 16(5): 563–86.

van Spanje, Joost, and Nan Dirk de Graaf (2018). "How Established Parties Reduce Other Parties' Electoral Support: The Strategy of Parroting the Pariah." *West European Politics* 41(1): 1–27.

Wagner, Markus (2021). "Affective Polarization in Multiparty Systems." *Electoral Studies* 69: 102199. https://doi.org/10.1016/j.electstud.2020.102199.

Weakliem, David L. (1993). "Class Conciousness and Political Change: Voting and Political Attitudes in the British Working Class, 1964 to 1970." *American Sociological Review* 58(3): 382–97.

Weisstanner, David, and Klaus Armingeon (2020). "How Redistributive Policies Reduce Market Inequality: Education Premiums in 22 OECD Countries." *Socio-Economic Review* 18(3): 839–56.

Westheuser, Linus (2021). "Pre-Political Bases of a New Cleavage: Social Identities, Moral Economy, and Classed Politics in Germany." Scuola Normale Superiore (Florence): PhD thesis.

Westheuser, Linus, and Delia Zollinger (2021). "Cleavage Theory Meets Bourdieu: Studying the Emergence of Cleavage Identities." Unpublished manuscript. https://doi.org/10.5167/uzh-213654.

Wlezien, Christopher, and Will Jennings (2023). "Institutions, Parties and the Evolution of Electoral Preferences." *European Journal of Political Research* 62: 1347–68. Online ahead of print. https://doi.org/10.1111/1475-6765.12579.

Wren, Anne, ed. (2013). *The Political Economy of the Service Transition.* Oxford: Oxford University Press.

Zald, Mayer N. (1996). "Culture, Ideology, and Strategic Framing." In *Comparative Perspectives on Social Movements: Political Opportunities, Mobilizing Structures, and Cultural Framings*, edited by Doug McAdam, John D. McCarthy, and Mayer N. Zald. Cambridge: Cambridge University Press, 261–74.

Zollinger, Delia (2022). "Status and Identity in Advanced Knowledge Societies – How Identity Construction and Political Contestation Counteract Status Concerns." Manuscript.

Zollinger, Delia (2023). "Place-based Identities and Cleavage Formation in the Knowledge Society." Manuscript.

Zollinger, Delia (2024). "Cleavage Identities in Voters' Own Words: Harnessing Open-Ended Survey Responses." *American Journal of Political Science* 68(1): 139–59.

Authors

Simon Bornschier directs the Research Area Political Sociology at the Department for Political Science at the University of Zurich. His research focuses on the formation and transformation of cleavages and party systems in Western Europe and South America, the varying degrees to which party systems represent the substantive preferences of voters, and the role of ideological polarization in this process. Personal homepage: www.simon-bornschier.eu.

Lukas Haffert is Associate Professor of Comparative Politics at the Department of Political Science, University of Geneva. His work focuses on processes of institutional change in advanced capitalist democracies, with a specific focus on historical processes of institution formation. Recent projects study fiscal policy, urban-rural divides and historical roots of political behavior. Personal homepage: www.lukashaffert.com

Silja Häusermann is Professor of Political Science at the University of Zurich in Switzerland. She studies welfare state politics and party system change in advanced capitalist democracies. She has directed the ERC-project "welfarepriorities" and is the co-director of the UZH University Research Priority Programme "Equality of Opportunity." Her work focuses on comparative political economy, inequality, comparative welfare state politics, and party system change in advanced capitalist democracies. Personal homepage: www.siljahaeusermann.org

Marco Steenbergen is Professor of Political Methodology at the University of Zurich in Switzerland. Methodologically, his primary research interests lie in choice models, machine learning, measurement, and multilevel analysis. Substantively, he is interested in political attitudes, beliefs, choices, identities, and values, as well as political parties. Personal homepage: www.steenbergen.ch

Delia Zollinger is a postdoctoral researcher at the Department of Political Science, University of Zurich. Her work focuses on long-term transformations of political conflict structures in knowledge economies, on how voters perceive their position in societies that are undergoing far-reaching economic and social change, and on how these perceptions relate to political attitudes and behavior. Personal homepage: www.deliazollinger.ch

Acknowledgement

This Element is the product of a cooperation between scholars working at the Department of Political Science at the University of Zurich. We dedicate it to our kind and lively scholarly community.

Cambridge Elements ≡

European Politics

Catherine De Vries
Bocconi University

Catherine De Vries is a Dean of International Affairs and Professor of Political Science at Bocconi University. Her research revolves around some of the key challenges facing the European continent today, such as Euroscepticism, political fragmentation, migration and corruption. She has published widely in leading political science journals, including the American Political Science Review and the Annual Review of Political Science. She has published several books, including Euroscepticism and the Future of European integration (Oxford University Press), received the European Union Studies Association Best Book in EU Studies Award, and was listed in the Financial Times top-5 books to read about Europe's future.

Gary Marks
University of North Carolina at Chapel Hill and European University Institute

Gary Marks is Burton Craige Professor at the University of North Carolina, Chapel Hill, and Professor at the European University Institute, Florence. He has received the Humboldt Forschungspreis and the Daniel Elazar Distinguished Federalism Scholar Award. Marks has been awarded an Advanced European Research Council grant (2010–2015) and is currently senior researcher on a second Advanced European Research Council grant. He has published widely in leading political science journals, including the American Political Science Review and the American Journal of Political Science. Marks has published a dozen books, including A Theory of International Organization and Community, Scale and Regional Governance.

Advisory Board
Sara Hobolt, *London School of Economics*
Sven-Oliver Proksch, *University of Cologne*
Jan Rovny, *Sciences Po, Paris*
Stefanie Walter, *University of Zurich*
Rahsaan Maxwell, *University of North Carolina, Chapel Hill*
Kathleen R. McNamara, *Georgetown University*
R. Daniel Kelemen, *Rutgers University*
Carlo Altomonte, *Bocconi University*

About the Series
The Cambridge Elements Series in European Politics will provide a platform for cutting-edge comparative research on Europe at a time of rapid change for the disciplines of political science and international relations. The series is broadly defined, both in terms of subject and academic discipline. The thrust of the series will be thematic rather than ideographic. It will focus on studies that engage key elements of politics – for example, how institutions work, how parties compete, how citizens participate in politics, how laws get made.

Cambridge Elements ≡

European Politics

Elements in the Series

Political Change and Electoral Coalitions in Western Democracies
Peter A. Hall, Georgina Evans and Sung In Kim

Cleavage Formation in the Twenty-First Century: How Social Identities Shape Voting Behavior in Contexts of Electoral Realignment
Simon Bornschier, Lukas Haffert, Silja Häusermann, Marco Steenbergen, and Delia Zollinger

A full series listing is available at: www.cambridge.org/EEP